The Invisible Journey

Daniel Koupermann C.

Dedication

This book is dedicated to my sons Jonathan, Joel, and Ilan, my best friends and sources of inspiration, as well as the most powerful manifestations of love in my life. To my granddaughter, Joseline, my new love.

Acknowledgments

To my three sons, for whose request this book was written.

To my beloved parents, Don Henry (Salomón) and Doña Yoly (Yolanda), who raised me and whose teachings and example I have followed to obtain a good life.

I also dedicate this book to Sarita, the mother of my children.

I dedicate this book to Linda, my wife, who has enabled me to experience love as a way of life through her generosity and presence.

To my teachers, Uwishins (Shamans-Healers) Tukupi, Mukuimbiu, Taish, and Sumpa, to Doña Amalia and Don Juan Arcos, and to the Salesian missionaries Raul de Vries and Luigi Bolla (Yankuam), all of whom made the Amazon a part of my skin and heart.

To Master George Ivanovich Gurdjieff, whose teachings allowed me to understand my mind and my relation with creation.

To Don Carlos Perez Perasso, who trusted in me and shared the dream that permitted the construction of Kapawi Ecolodge, my life's most outstanding project, which has successfully protected thousands of hectares and the culture of the Achuar in the Ecuadorian Amazon.

To John Perkins, Bill, and Lynne Twist, with whom I have worked for decades, facilitating personal transformations and obtaining resources for nature conservation and the well-being of specific ancestral Latin American populations.

To the Tatas Domingo and Julio Tot in Guatemala, and to my colleagues German Canales in Peru and Jaruen and Lucy Rodriguez in Colombia, who have contributed to making the trips I offer a life experience for me and my friends and clients.

To life itself that has given me so much...

To Ariel Dawi, for the exceptional cover design that beautifully captures the spirit and essence of this book.
To life itself that has given me so much…

About the Author

My academic background is in business administration with a specialty in Hotel Management. I was involved in this field for the first 12 years of my career, working with my father, who owned several hotels in Cuenca and on the coast of Ecuador. Then it was time to make a change. I began working with a tour operator in the adventure travel business specializing in Indigenous cultures, birdwatching, orchids, archeology, and the rainforest. I spent 12 years in the Amazon rainforest in the Shuar territory.

Next, I was contacted by a tourism corporation in Quito, which had a large cruise ship in the Galapagos Islands. The owner of the corporation asked me to develop an upscale lodge in the Amazon Region of Ecuador. Over the next 2 years, I oversaw the construction of the Kapawi Lodge and the development of the concept for a low-impact Amazon lodge. We used (for the first time in Ecuador) photovoltaic installation and 4-stroke outboard engines. We developed protocols to work with the Achuar communities and to use ecotourism as a powerful nature conservancy tool. Also, this project was conceived under a very special equation for a business project at that time, 1994. The corporation invested 1.7 million US dollars to build the Lodge, without buying the land, and committed to returning the ongoing business to the Indigenous people after 15 years of operation. This was considered enough time for the corporation to get a return on its investment and for the Achuar to learn how to manage and operate the lodge and the tourism operation. Everything happened as planned, and the lodge is today fully owned and managed by the Achuar. The Kapawi Lodge has become a powerful conservation tool and has brought an economic system to the territory, giving the Achuar an economic development alternative.

During the final stages of building the Lodge, I became involved in the creation of The Pachamama Alliance Foundation, a US-based NGO. I was President of the Pachamama Foundation in Ecuador for 15 years.

After managing the Lodge for 5 years, I was asked to work on a cruise ship in the Galapagos Islands, owned by the same company that funded the construction of the Kapawi Lodge. My mission on the cruise ship was to improve service quality and develop a community-based operation on Isabela Island.

After finishing my job on the cruise ship, I took a sabbatical year and traveled all around Ecuador, visiting small towns and gathering information for a popular calendar of festivals. After my sabbatical, I was hired by The Pachamama Alliance in the US to develop and manage a new air service on the edge of the Amazon jungle, specifically for the Achuar. The main goal for me was to educate and coach the Achuar to take on management of the air service themselves. I spent 2 1/2 years managing the Achuar Air Service (Aerotsentsak), developing administrative tools and operational daily practices, and training the Achuar to use these tools and practices to successfully manage the fleet of 3 airplanes and pilots.

Then, in 2012, I restarted my travel business, offering holistic trips for personal growth and healing, rooted in the traditional knowledge and practices of Indigenous cultures. My trips are in Guatemala with the Mayans, in Peru with the Queros, in Colombia with the Kogis, and in Ecuador with the Kichua Karanquis in the Andes and the Achuar in the Amazon. I also take trips to Patagonia, starting in Argentina and ending in Chile. This is the only journey where I do not have direct contact with indigenous people due to the hard conditions in which the Mapuche and the Guarani live. In this journey, the beauty of Nature is the healer. The name of my travel company is ANDEAN PATHS (www.andeanpathsjourneys.com).

In my free time, I am an advisor to Corporación Ecológica Tierra Viva, a local NGO based in my city, Cuenca. Tierra Viva's mission is to provide environmental education and raise awareness of the threats nature faces from extractive activities and the harmful practices of our societies, which affect the balance and future of Mother Earth.

Since 2024, I have been a member of the board of directors of Director of CDS (Sustainable Development Corporation), an NGO that develops and implements sustainable projects.

I am also a consultant in eco-lodge design and operation, with low-impact practices.

I am living in Cuenca with my wife, Linda. I am a father to 3 sons, ages 33, 40, and 42. I am a grandfather to an 11-year-old girl.

Table of Contents

Foreword
by John Perkins

Daniel Koupermann has lived an extraordinary life. It's the kind of life young people who read romantic adventure classics like *Treasure Island*, more modern fantasies like *Harry Potter*, or the latest science fiction and superhero books dream of having. And yet only a few of the most intrepid, persevering, and astute people could actually live and survive this type of life. As you will see in these pages, Daniel follows the tradition of legendary heroes like Marco Polo, Daniel Boone, Ernest Shackleton, and David Livingstone.

I first met Daniel when he was around 10 years old, and I was in my early twenties. I was a US Peace Corps volunteer assigned to the Shuar Territory deep in the Ecuadorian Amazon rainforest. Following Peace Corps policy, every month I made the arduous journey from the jungle to check in at a Peace Corps office in the Andean city of Cuenca (at 8,000 feet). This involved hours of slugging through the mud of treacherous jungle trails, usually soaked to the skin by drenching rain, and then catching a ride on a rickety bus full of campesinos, chickens, pigs, and the occasional goat, as it wound its way up the rutted muck of a serpentine dirt road to the mountain town of Gualaceo. There, I had to spend the cold Andean night at what was called an "inn." The room was bare except for a filthy mattress, a thin blanket, and a wobbly table that held a porcelain pitcher and wash basin. To get to the bathroom—a dilapidated privy about fifty feet from the house—I had to pick my way down slippery outside wooden stairs. The next day was another ride on a bus, only slightly better than the previous one, to Cuenca.

Perhaps it should come as no surprise that on one such journey, I developed a severe sore throat and a high fever. Early in the morning after a feverish night, I found myself walking the town's muddy street, hoping to find a pharmacy, when a jeep pulled up beside me. A middle-aged man stuck his head through the window and shouted, "Can I give you a ride?"

I'd heard of Henry Koupermann. He was the owner of the best hotel in Cuenca (one we Peace Corps volunteers could not afford). But I had no idea that he also owned a luxurious resort just outside Gualaceo that catered to wealthy families from Cuenca and other cities. That day, he took me to his resort and nursed me back to health. It was the beginning of a friendship that eventually introduced me to his 10-year-old son, Daniel.

Many years later, I returned to Ecuador. I hoped to rectify some of the damage I had done in my job as chief economist ("economic hit man") at a Boston-based consulting firm by helping the Shuar protect their territory. Their lands, some of the most biodiverse in the world, were being devastated by oil and mining companies that benefited from the hydroelectric dams, roads, and other infrastructure I had helped develop. I went looking for Henry. Although he had died, I was led to Daniel, who, as fate would have it, owned an eco-tourist business and was highly respected by the Shuar.

I explained to Daniel that for nearly a decade, I had believed that the work I was doing as chief economist was good for the majority of Ecuadorians and those in other countries where I'd worked. I had been taught in business school and by the World Bank that building such infrastructure projects increased gross domestic product per capita. While statistically speaking, that is true, over time, I'd come to understand that GDP primarily measures the wealth of the richest families and their corporations. GDP per capita may sound like it indicates how well the majority of the people are doing, but that is extremely deceptive. GDP per capita is simply GDP divided by the total number of people in the country. I told Daniel that once I'd learned this, I'd quit and was devoting the rest of my life to exposing and changing the system I had previously promoted. I wanted to return to the Shuar. He offered to help.

The Shuar, like many Amazonian people, are a dream culture. They understood that it wasn't really the oil and mining companies that were destroying the rainforest and the rest of the world as we know it; it was the dream of the people who consume the products of oil and mining companies. They asked Daniel and me to bring people from that world to learn from them about the importance of changing the dream of those who were in the process of driving humanity to the edge of self-destruction. That was back in the late 1980s. Ever since, Daniel and I have brought people from many countries to learn from the Shuar about how to "change the dream of the modern world."

You will learn from this book that, as I said, Daniel has lived an extraordinary life. He is an adventurer, environmentalist, advocate for indigenous rights, and social and economic change, and... Well, that will come when you read his words.

First, there is one thing more I want to say: if I am in a dangerous situation, there is no one I'd want by my side more than Daniel Koupermann. And he has been there, time and again. Here is just one example.

I was flying in a small plane to meet him in the Achuar Territory, accompanied by Yahanua, a Shuar woman; Ehud Sperling, the founder and CEO of Inner Traditions International and the publisher of my five books on Indigenous cultures; and Juan Gabriel Carrasco, an Ecuadorian travel guide who worked with Daniel and me. The four of us had spent the previous night with Tukupi, a Shuar elder who was reputed to have killed more Achuar than any other living Shuar during the wars that had ended years earlier. He was also Yahanua's godfather. What follows is excerpted from *Touching the Jaguar*.

Now it was 1993, and I was trapped in a small Cessna on a muddy airstrip, staring out at spear-waving, face-painted Achuar warriors who were screaming "Kill! Kill! Kill!" Their spears banged against the plane's thin metal fuselage.

"Just take off," I yelled at the petrified pilot.

"I can't," he screamed back. "They've stuck logs in front of my wheels."

"Kill Yahanua! Kill Tukupi's daughter!"

"Kill! Kill Yahanua! Kill Tukupi's daughter!"

Word had travelled fast, and now we were surrounded by warriors whose fathers and brothers had been killed by Tukupi and whose code of honor demanded that they kill Yahanua and, probably, the three of us who had travelled with her to Tukupi.

Daniel's tall frame pushed through the seething crowd. I wondered if they would kill him, too.

He finally made it to the plane and raised his hands. "Brothers, let me speak," he shouted in Spanish. Someone translated it into Achuar. Surprisingly, the chanting stopped. "These people are my friends." He motioned for the pilot to shut down the engine. "They come in peace."

Inside the plane, the clicking of a seatbelt and the sound of the latch on the door next to Juan Gabriel. I struggled to release my own seatbelt. The door opened, and Daniel's hand reached in. "Come quickly," he said to Juan Gabriel.

I was next, the sun blinding me as I stumbled to the ground and was held up by Daniel's firm hand on my arm. I turned to watch Ehud step out.

As his foot touched the ground, the silence was shattered by a hair-raising scream.

One of the warriors rushed toward the open doorway.

Daniel quickly stepped between him and the plane. The warrior stopped inches from Daniel and glared at him. Daniel spoke to him softly and, at the same time, shut the plane's door.

The Achuar men closed in around the three of us as we huddled close to Daniel. Shaking their spears, they resumed chanting, "Kill, kill Yahanua."

Daniel's hands went up. Once again, silence. His manner and his voice, calm, controlled, and yet firm, had an immediate impact on the Achuar. They lowered their spears and listened.

"Those are the old ways," he said. "The Achuar and Shuar are no longer at war. Now, you must all join together: Achuar, Shuar, Quichua—all the nations—to fight your common enemy, the oil and mining companies." He touched my shoulder. "This is John

Perkins. I've told you about him and his organization, Dream Change. He is here to help you."

The ground beneath my feet was spinning as Daniel ushered Ehud, Juan Gabriel, and me to the shade of a nearby tree. I watched him return to the mob of warriors. I caught a brief glimpse of a phantom face peering through the plane's window. Yahanua.

After minutes that seemed like hours, there was commotion near the plane. The Achuar warriors milled around it for a while and then slowly backed away. Daniel came to us.

"I couldn't convince them to let her stay." He shrugged his shoulders. "She'll have to leave."

"Alive?" One of us asked.

"Yes."

The pilot had already started the engine. Slowly, the plane began to turn around. The wind of the propeller spattered us with mud. The pilot revved the engine.

As we watched it race down the runway, we waved. It picked up speed, lifted off, and flew over the trees.

I felt relief that Yahanua would return unharmed to her own people. I also found myself wishing that I were on that plane with her.

"Traditions are hard to break," Daniel said.

He led us down a narrow, muddy trail to the wide Pastaza River. We stood for a moment staring at the turbulent waters that had plummeted down from Andean glaciers and were on their long journey to the Atlantic.

It's important to point out that today the Achuar and Shuar are united in a partnership that also includes other indigenous nations, the Pachamama Alliance, and many international organizations that are committed to protecting this essential part of the world, known as the Sacred Headwaters of the Amazon. Some of the young Achuar men who attacked our plane are instrumental to that partnership. And some are now married to Shuar women. This remarkable reversal of hostile traditions that endured for thousands of years offers a deeply encouraging model for countries around the planet to come together to fight a common enemy: our current lifestyles and the goal of maximizing materialist consumption and short-term profits. Daniel has been one of the most important agents of change in this process.

But enough from me. Now, his story. . .

* **John Perkins** is the author of eleven books on shamanism, economics, and transformation, including *Touching the Jaguar, Shapeshifting,* and *Confessions of an Economic Hit Man,* which is published in 38 languages and has spent more than 70 weeks on *The New York Times* bestseller list.

Foreword
by Lynne Twist

Over my lifetime, I've had the great privilege of knowing and working with some of the most remarkable people on this planet. I had the profound privilege of working side by side with Mother Teresa in India, and I have also spent time in deep meditation and in collaboration with His Holiness the Dalai Lama. I was blessed enough to be in South Africa to attend Nelson Mandela's inauguration, and after that, I worked closely with Archbishop Desmond Tutu. I've had the honor of working with the Nobel Women's Peace Prize laureates, including Jody Williams, Leymah Gbowee, Shirin Ebadi, Wangari Maathai, and other remarkable women who overcame impossible odds to contribute to peace and the well-being of people all over the world.

In my work to end hunger and the oppression of women and girls, I've known and worked with many courageous souls and extraordinary beings whose names are not well known, but who lived lives with grace, dignity, and reverence in soul-crushing, harsh, and unforgiving circumstances. Their courage and heart have deeply informed and inspired my life.

However, one of the greatest and most amazing human beings I've ever had the privilege to know and work with is Daniel Koupermann. He is a mentor, a spiritual teacher, a wisdom keeper, and a soul brother to me and my husband, Bill Twist. He has lived an extraordinary life and made a phenomenal difference in the lives of thousands of people. I am one of them.

In 1995, Bill and I were so fortunate to be led deep into the Amazon rainforest of Ecuador by Daniel and John Perkins, where we had our first encounter with the Achuar people. Daniel and John had worked together for many years, and Daniel had become a revered and respected Ecuadorian guide as well as a deeply trusted ally for the indigenous peoples of the Amazon and the Andes. That encounter in the rainforest led to the creation of the Pachamama Alliance, an organization co-founded by John Perkins, Bill, and me that has supported the indigenous people for decades in protecting their lands and cultures.

But there would not have been a Pachamama Alliance without Daniel Koupermann. He has worked side by side with us for the past 30 years, opening every door we walked through in Ecuador and Peru. Daniel introduced us to the key leaders of each of the indigenous nations we have worked with, and their trust and respect for him have made our work possible. Because of that trust, we have been able to support and empower nearly 30 Indigenous nations to come together to form the Amazon Sacred Headwaters Alliance, an unprecedented collaboration working to preserve the Amazon rainforest in this time of great threat to that critical global ecosystem.

Early in life, Daniel was a hotelier, and later, as the designer and builder of Kapawi Ecolodge, he was responsible for turning ecotourism into a tool for the conservation of the Amazon forest. He has guided travelers all over Central and South America and has opened thousands of hearts and minds to the cultures of indigenous people. His work with indigenous people has taught him perhaps the deepest lessons a human being can learn—open-heartedness, humility, respect, and love for Nature and community.

In this fascinating autobiography, Daniel tells the story of his own family, his parents and grandparents, and how he came to be such an extraordinarily powerful and wise human being. He shares stories of his years of adventures in the forest with jungle animals, shamans, and plant medicines, where he gained the knowledge and experience to become both a businessman and a naturalist expedition leader.

The many twists and turns of his life have been both beautiful and challenging, devastating and exhilarating, and always received by him as teaching. His commitment to his own interior growth and development, his wholeness and integrity, and his willingness to release any kind of agenda other than service have always been deeply inspiring to me and my husband, Bill.

For 30 years now, Daniel has had a huge and important presence in my life. I was thrilled when Daniel fell in love with and married one of my closest and dearest friends, Linda Leyerle. Their marriage of many years warms my heart and soul. She is an amazing partner for Daniel and has embraced his whole family, and they have embraced her.

In the book, Daniel shares eloquently about his many personal passages. All of what he has written is transparent and inspiring. From his incredible life, he draws many lessons and shares the teachings that he considers "essential for understanding vital situations in our lives."

It was such an honor to read this beautiful book, to know more of the history of this remarkable man, and to reflect on his wisdom and insights. You are about to embark on an engaging and poignant journey with a very special human being. Enjoy the ride!

***Lynne Twist**

Co-Founder, Pachamama Alliance

President and Founder, The Soul of Money Institute

Author of *Soul of Money* and *Living a Committed Life.*

INTRODUCTION

My initial intention for writing my memoirs was to respond to my children's requests. Since they were little, I have shared the stories of my trips and life. One day, as I was with them, they told me, "Pa, we want to ask you to write your memoirs, the stories you have shared with us throughout the years. We want you to leave them in writing to remember and pass on those stories to our children."

This request resonated profoundly because it gave a unique value to an essential part of their upbringing since they were little. Thus, I decided to leave part of my life story and the story of my ancestors to my children. Share with them the events of life and the course of my history. With this intention, I started to write about my known origins, which go back to my maternal and paternal grandparents.

Little by little, going down memory lane, there was a moment when I decided to read what I had written. I was astounded and overwhelmed by how incredibly diverse, wonderful, and intense my life has been. There has been so much learning, books read, and sights seen. There have been so many paths taken, so many people met, so much music heard and danced, so many trips, so much philosophy, so much knowledge, so much life... so much of everything. What a life!!

When I looked at it from this perspective, I connected with one of the most critical lessons learned: " The Invisible Journey", which appears in the book Tahuantinsuyo 5.0 written by the Peruvian master healer Alonso del Rio, who lives in the Sacred Valley of Pisac in Peru.

"The idea is that there are two journeys in one's life: one-way and return. The first trip is the visible journey, and the return trip is the invisible journey. The first is a trip toward diversity, and the other a trip toward unity; one toward the mind and the other toward the heart; one toward knowledge and the other toward wisdom.

You can feel the invisible journey when your intuition tells you that you have arrived at the end of the first journey. Where else to search? How much more information do you want to acquire? How big will you allow your ego to grow before offering it?"

It is based on the dynamic principle between love and suffering. Every time we love, our capacity to suffer expands, and every time we suffer, our capacity to love expands. Thus, the strength of our capacity to love equals the force of our capacity to suffer. They grow together and are complementary to each other. They don't depend on our will or conscience; they simply happen as a condition particular to our species.

Love and pain are the two wings given to us at the end of the first path, without which it is impossible to fly back. The invisible journey has no rules or time; if you see it, you have already done it. There is no way to prepare for it and do it better because you don't walk; you fly. Although there is no difference between the goal and you, you still fly. There is no way to learn it. You must know it; your flight depends on the size and potency of your wings, love, and pain.

Then, I understood that my memoirs were the details of my first visible journey. This journey was where I accumulated knowledge, experimented with love and suffering in many forms, and built my beliefs. It was also the journey where my mind dominated my perception of life and the construction of my ego, thanks to which I have been able to survive and navigate through life.

This is where the name of the book "The Invisible Journey" comes from. An idea to understand our lives. It encourages readers to look at their own lives, to remember their one-way trip and their visible trip, and to reflect upon the moment to initiate their return journey, the journey toward unity, wisdom, and the heart.

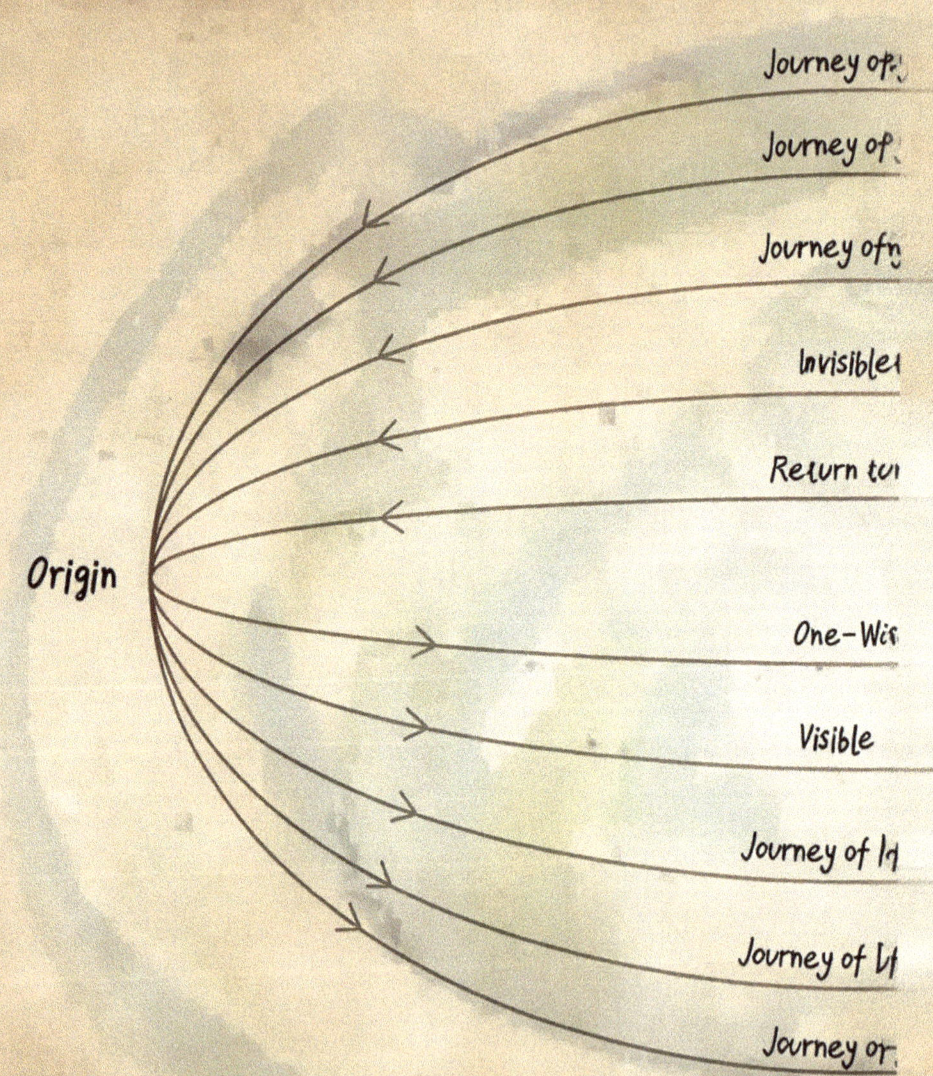

Origin
Journey of
Journey of
Journey of
Invisible
Return to
One-Wis
Visible
Journey of l
Journey of l
Journey of

the Heart
Unity
Wisdom
Journey
the Origin
y Journey
Journey
Knowledge
Diversity
the Mind
ego
love
suffering

1. The Origin

My grandfather, Yitzhak, was born in August 1877 in Uman, a city in Cherkasy Oblast, Central Ukraine. His parents settled in Odesa, on the shores of the Black Sea, in response to an edict issued by Tsar Alexander I of Russia that invited Germans to colonize the area. The group is known as the Black Sea Germans.

Yitzhak joined Tsar Nicholas's army, a rare condition for a Jew at the time. The 1905 pogrom against the Jews in Odessa was the most severe pogrom of that period, with more than 2500 Jews assassinated. My grandfather had to emigrate to Argentina, protected by Baron Mauricio de Hirsch's initiative, who helped emigrate jews to Argentina. This originated the Jewish Colonization Association, founded in London by Baron De Hirsch (1891). This philanthropic organization aimed to facilitate immigration to Argentina and Palestine for several decades. Its purpose was to create agricultural colonies. Yitzhak must have arrived there with his wife Ana between 1892 and 1895. They had three sons, Mauricio, Gregorio, and Bernardo. Then, in 1905, they emigrated to France as political refugees. He settled in Drancy (a Parisian neighborhood), selling fruit from a horse and carriage and having two more sons, Salomon, my father (November 6, 1913), and Ramon. On my father's birth certificate, you can see that my grandfather's trade was a fruit merchant, and the witnesses are Alexander Hassan, the tailor, and Theodore Rubenstein, the shoemaker.

Through a matchmaker, the Jewish community in Paris facilitated Salomon's wedding to Sara, an immigrant girl from Poland, with whom he had a daughter, Paulette. When the girl was born, they emigrated to Barranquilla, Colombia, because his older brother, Maurice, resided in Cartagena. There, he installed a hat factory.

Once France fell under the Nazi army, my father enlisted in the French foreign resistance, organized around General De Gaulle from June 18, 1940, which encompassed the Free French Forces. In 1943, he adhered to the French Committee for National Liberation in Algiers and became part of the French Liberation Army. He fought alongside the Allied forces until all French territories were liberated. After the liberation of France, fed up with the war and having lost his family and friends in the Holocaust, he decided to return to Colombia in search of his wife and daughter. He sails across the North Atlantic to Panama, where he sends telegrams to his brothers Maurice in Colombia and Gregorio in Buenos Aires to announce his return, and that's when he finds out that his wife Sara sold his factory and went to France with his daughter Paulette, who was three years old, searching for him. He was deeply depressed by the news and didn't understand why Sarah had made such a foolish decision. The consequences for

Sara and Paulette were grave because they had to survive by hiding from the Nazis, who were searching for Jews to send to the concentration camps. With the help of good people, they escaped to Holland, to Franco's Spain, and finally back to Colombia. Salomon and Sara never met again. Paulette saw her father in 1959 when she visited Ecuador; I was 1 year old.

When Salomon found out what his wife had done, he continued his trip toward Buenos Aires on the Pacific coast to Chile. His plan was to cross the Cordillera and arrive in Argentina. The ship dropped anchor in Guayaquil for five days to get provisions and water, which allowed Salomon to walk around the city's streets. He was attracted by the enormous rubber and mango trees, dirt streets, and the grand porches in front of the houses. He slept on a park bench for two nights in Parque Seminario. When he woke up on the second day, he was surprised to find an exquisite gentleman standing before the bench. When he asked what he wanted, the gentleman just answered that his attention was caught by the sight of someone sleeping in the park and asked where he was from. Salomon explained that he had come from France, from the war, to which the gentleman exclaimed in perfect French that he had lived in Paris before the war and had a house he had abandoned due to the international conflict. This man was Juan X Marcos, the wealthiest man in Ecuador in those days, owner of the largest coffee and cocoa plantations. He invited my father to stay in Ecuador, arguing that the country needed foreigners to develop. When he asked my father about his trade, he told him about his hat factory and that before that, he had worked as a cook in various restaurants, to which Juan X Marcos replied that Guayaquil lacked a French food restaurant and that it would be an excellent idea for him to stay and open one. Salomon pointed out his lack of money to do it, and J X Marcos answered no to worry because he would help him, and to please stay in Guayaquil.

That is how my father opened his first French restaurant in Guayaquil, "Henry's," next to the United States consulate on 9 de Octubre Avenue. In those days, the consulate was very active and busy because there was an American Air Force base in Baltra in the Galapagos Islands. The restaurant was a total success. Finally, the aristocracy from Guayaquil and the American military had a place where they could eat well: Chateaubriand, filet mignon, onion soup, rabbit in mushroom sauce, coquille Saint Jacques, coq au vin, thermidor lobster, Florentine eggs, sea bass with seafood sauce, calamari in Provenzale sauce, rollmops, and others. He maintained those same recipes throughout his hotel career. Since that moment, Salomon adopted the name Henry, which was more consistent with his French restaurant, and made it his new name, Henry Koupermann (As it was registered in France when my grandfather arrived as a political refugee).

There was a German pilot who had fled from Nazi Germany and worked as a pilot for Juan X Marcos, flying his biplane to visit the farms and plantations on the Ecuadorian coast. A great friendship developed between the German pilot and Henry. Occasionally, they would borrow the airplane on weekends to go to Salinas. Back then, there were no roads, and you could only reach the beach by boat or train.

During one of those trips, they landed on Salinas Beach. Henry met Yolanda, a beautiful criolla woman with a long black braid, surfing the waves on a yola (narrow wooden canoe) around the rocks where the Salinas Yacht Club Marina now lies. They fell in love madly, and in 1953, they married and moved to Guayaquil. After five years of marriage, I was born...my origin.

On the maternal side, our origins go back to the Spanish, who arrived during colonial times and adapted to life in the Andean mountains. They settled in Ambato and became landowners and agricultural merchants. My grandfather was Pedro Carrera, and my grandmother was Marina Montenegro Villalba.

2. My Visible Trip, One-Way Trip: Childhood and Adolescence

Memories from my childhood and adolescence are happy memories. Some moments in my fragile memory have been recorded and, in some way, have marked me forever.

My parents had two children after me—my sister Giselle del Carmen and Jean Claude. My childhood's happy memories go back to when we were young and living in Cuenca (1961 to 1965). School, friends, family, weekends at our country house, La Hostería Gualaceo, cows, chickens, ducks, geese, rabbits, escargots, fish, canaries and Australian parakeets, pears, apples, passion fruit, reina claudias, satsumas, black cherries, alfalfa, palms, dates, and my mare Floreana. We would return to Cuenca on Sundays after lunch and start the ritual: bathing, getting the clothes and school supplies, and getting into our parents' bed to watch Daktari on TV while eating churrasco with fries. We traveled to our house on the beach, Hosteria Samarina, for vacations, where, later, we would live for some years; the sea, beautiful sunsets, waves, tides, fishermen, sun, sand, heat… a natural, happy, and complete world.

On December 5, 1963, Jean Claude was born. He was a beautiful blue boy who was born with inverted heart arteries, so his life was very fragile. At that time, medicine hadn't developed enough to solve my little brother's problem. The doctors told my parents that they had to wait until he was 10 years old to have surgery and that the way to keep him alive was to live at sea level because Cuenca, our city, is located at 2600 meters (8530 feet) above sea level.

In 1964, when I was 7 years old, while playing golf, I was accidentally hit in my head, which caused a severe craniocerebral concussion. Some splintered skull bones landed on the encephalic mass, which could cause the risk of bruising certain vulnerable areas, which would eventually affect the speech or cause movement deficiencies and other risks inherent to the seriousness of the case. I was taken to the emergency room of Santa Ana Clinic, where Dr. Vicente Corral Moscoso, a surgeon, performed the surgery. My parents had to sign a document exempting the doctors and the clinic from responsibility in case of collateral damage or death. The 5-and-a-half-hour surgery was a total success carried out by the virtuous hands of Dr. Vicente and his team. An observation period of 72 hours was determined to confirm the recuperation of all the functions. Big surprise! After 72 hours, I had a chickenpox crisis, which covered my body with intolerable, itchy blisters. I remember my loving mother blowing on my body to calm the itchiness, representing a sublime manifestation of her love. I felt totally loved. In the same manner, my classmates from school sent cards made by them, filled with lovely drawings, wishing me a prompt recovery. All my classmates went to the Clinic's street, and when I looked out the window, they were waving their hands and expressing their love through movements and facial expressions. The golf accident and the chickenpox crisis opened a powerful portal through which I experimented with unforgettable expressions of love and care.

My parents went to the coast to find a place to live and allow for the survival of my little brother. They bought land (1964), where they built the Hotel Samarina. They were successful, making it into the favorite place for lunch or dinner for families from Guayaquil to spend their vacations in Salinas. Families from the highlands would always visit on their vacations or holidays. It was a piece of paradise with great hosts—my parents. Jean Claude was growing up well, which made us hopeful that he would make it to his 10th birthday and be cured of his illness. He became quite a character among the visitors because he was always by my father's side in his little pedal car. At the same time, Henry made his rounds through the tables, greeting the clients and ensuring everything was as they wished. Jean Claude copied my father and asked the guests about the taste of the food. He was a beautiful little person, and everyone adored him.

These years on the coast laid the foundations of my relationship with the ocean. Watching the sea daily, the flocks of pelicans in large formations, and listening to the waves were part of my everyday life. I remember three particular events from that time.

The first one is going with my mother to gather barnacles in Punta Carnero. My mom would tie a rope around me and attach it to her waist, and we would go to the place where the waves crashed onto the rocks by the shore. When the waves crashed, we would duck, and while the wave was retreating, we would quickly gather all the barnacles and place them in a net that was also tied to my mother's body. It was exciting and risky, but my mother's confidence was transmitted, and I was thrilled. Then, at home, we would eat the barnacles with my father and sister. Knowing where they came from, it was a moment of great satisfaction.

Another memory involves my mother as the protagonist. We would fight the waves on high tide on the Hotel's beach. She taught me how to do it, and I became an expert in battling 3-meter-high waves at a very young age. The Hotel's guests would gather on the restaurant's terrace to watch me fight the waves.

The other thing I remember with great attachment was swimming to the rock island in front of the Hotel at low tide to dive and get sea urchins, which I would bring back to my father. He loved to eat fresh sea urchins. He would open them in the center, and with a small coffee spoon, he would pick up the yellow substance, put some lemon drops and some mustard, and bon appetit! I felt thrilled to be able to offer my father this little pleasure.

My father decided to extend the Samarina hotel and build the first 5-star hotel on the Ecuadorian coast after seeing his business's success and falling in love with Ecuador.

Part of the development project was to build a Marina for yachts and sailboats, so he requested permission from the Ecuadorian Navy and the La Libertad municipality to be granted the private use of the beach, which was granted. He built a wall to mark the hotel's beach, which was poorly understood by the town politicians who protested that concession. There are many beaches in that zone; nevertheless, they used my father's project for their own political interests and organized a demonstration against the "gringo" who wanted to take away one of their beaches. Many people arrived at the hotel beach, shouting harangues against the gringo. At that moment, Jean Claude played with his babysitter at the beach, so the babysitter ran towards the house. The child was frightened by the scandal and the shouting. The protesters placed dynamite on the wall, and pieces of rock blew everywhere; many fell on the house, perforating the ceiling.

My mother was desperately screaming due to the moment's violence. She placed my sister and me under the bed and took my little brother in her arms to protect us while the rocks kept coming in through the roof and the windows. Her terrified shrieks and the detonations were the only sounds we could hear. My little brother was so frightened that his heart did not resist, and he died.... He was only 3 years old (1966). My parents screamed in desperate impotence, rage, and pain, understanding that my little brother had died. Upon seeing my parents in that state, I ran out of the house, trying to escape from the scene, which for me was unbearable. I was 8 years old and ran madly, not knowing where to escape. Suddenly, I found myself in the Hotel's restaurant kitchen; I opened the oven door and lay inside in a fetal position for a long time until one of the hotel employees found me and took me back to my parents, who hugged me and couldn't stop crying. Their facial expression was one of sadness and grief that I would never forget. In my future life, every time I have suffered profoundly, this image comes to my mind.

We continued living at Samarina, and my father continued with his project of building a 5-star hotel, where he was economically prosperous and where his little Jean Claude died.

3. I am a Jew!!

The construction of the new project advanced, and we had to move to a new house at the entrance to the property because the new hotel occupied the whole front of the cliffs above the beach. It was our custom to kiss our parents each time we arrived home from school. When I went down to my parents' bedroom, I found my father sitting on the edge of the bed, crying. I was surprised, and as I approached to greet him, I asked him why he was crying. Was he sick? He told me that he was crying with anger and sadness because Arab countries had attacked Israel (1967, the Six-Day War), which was the country of the Jews. Since he was a Jew, this abusive and disproportionate attack hurt him immensely. This was the first time in my life that I learned that my father was a Jew. For me, it was an unexpected revelation because, at the same time, he told me about his story as an ex-fighter of the Second World War. From that moment, there was a significant change in my identity. I felt Jewish like my father, identifying with him as my hero. I had attended catholic nuns and priests' schools, as well as evangelical schools, and I had heard, throughout my childhood, unpleasant stories about the Jews. At my parents' house, there was an agreement between them regarding our religious education: they agreed that the only religion they would teach us was the Ten Commandments, about which they discussed and gave examples.

My father invested all his money, and at some point, he had to look for investors to continue the project. The most viable option was to associate with a group of investors from Guayaquil who had already built two hotels in Salinas (Miramar and Punta Carnero). For some reason, my father didn't feel comfortable with this group. Thus, he decided to associate with the Ecuadorian State, forming one of the first mixed economy companies, public and private. There was a long-term friendship with Dr. Jose Maria Velasco Ibarra, the President of the country. The association with the State worked well, and the project advanced diligently. The construction ended, and they worked on the final details and equipment.

On February 15, 1972, a coup d'état overthrew Dr. José María Velasco Ibarra. This historical event, known as the "carnavalazo," ended in the instauration of a military dictatorship headed by General Guillermo Rodríguez Lara. Consequently, the dictatorship intervened in the Mixed Economy Company between Henry Koupermann and the National Direction of Tourism (DITURIS), representing the State. After a very long investigative process, a final report was obtained by the General Comptroller's office of the Republic, when General Solon Espinoza was General Comptroller, in which the legal status of the Mixed Economy Company was confirmed and its processes and advances. During the investigation, which lasted over a year, there were abuses and manipulation of due process, and the culmination of the project, which had an advance of 95%, was paralyzed. This intervention did not permit credit (loan) payments from Banco La

Previsora. After a waiting period, the Bank auctioned Hotel Samarina and all the goods my dad had accumulated until that date. It was a financial, emotional, and family catastrophe. We lost all of our family patrimony. The expropriation of my father's goods was known to public opinion, and it was qualified as one of the "great injustices" committed during the military dictatorship. Articulo El Universo 1973/Alfredo Pinoargote.

The only business he kept was Hotel Cuenca, registered under my mother's name, with which we survived our family's catastrophe. In that state of things and with my father profoundly affected by the loss of his son and the whole patrimony constructed with years of effort, some friends from Banco del Azuay, who knew the story, offered my father the opportunity to buy the famous Hotel Crespo, because there were irreversible misunderstandings among the heirs of Don Luis Heredia Crespo. The Bank offered a mortgage loan to buy the hotel and improve the infrastructure and equipment. The opportunity to initiate a project again without having any money was a blessing (1973). He gathered his strength and once again constructed a stable and prestigious business based on his personality as a great host and the excellent French food that always characterized him.

For me, this was one of the most important lessons from my father. Having received such a strong blow with the loss of his son, his fortune, and his dream, he found the inspiration to raise his spirit, his strength, and his inner peace in us (his wife and two children).

4. Adolescence

I spent part of my teen years in Cuenca (1972 to 1974) with an average life: studying in high school again, sports, parties, girlfriends, friends, and a few very close friends who left an indelible mark of brotherhood.

It was a time of experimentation with psychotropic substances, marijuana, Quaalude pills, mandrax, lysergic acid, ethyl chloride, San Pedro cactus (*echinoid pachanoi*), and Sylosibium mushrooms. There were so many experiences with drugs and with friends from all walks of life, from those of the high class to those shunned by society. I got along well with all of them. One of the clearest memories was when I rode my mare Floreana from Hosteria Gualaceo to a property in Bullcay, where my friend, known as the Lora (parrot) Rodas, lived. We organized a cactus San Pedro (*Echinopsis pachanoi)* drinking ceremony. The Lora had slow-cooked it in a ceramic pot the night before under a full moon. We drank the brew, and when the effect took hold, we went into the river with its silver water by the moonlight. We sang and enjoyed a spectacular moment filled with physical feelings of lightness and connection with the elements.

Late that night, as I was getting ready to return, I saw, by the shore where the cactus had been cooked, an essential amount of solids sifted from the concoction and placed on the pot again. I made pieces of a raw cane sugar tablet I always brought for Floreana and mixed it with what was left in the pot. I gave it to Floreana, who happily ate it. After a long while, I started my trip back on the edge of the road. The moon had disappeared, and the sky was alight with stars; I occasionally saw the lights of other cars that came in the opposite direction. Suddenly, I concentrated on the horse's neck movements with its long mane, which moved rhythmically to the beat of the rhythm of her constant gallop. The stars were all over, above and below us. Floreana was flying in the middle of a starry sky; the wind and freshness covered my face. The sensation of flying on my horse remained until I arrived home. It was so real and vivid that it was one of the most beautiful experiences that I've had with psychotropics in my life.

The experience with different states of consciousness was a profound learning experience about society and myself. These experiences created a feeling of "not belonging" to anything—a profound solitude. For my parents, getting me out of the influence of the circle I frequented in Cuenca became a priority. During those days, a family from Cartagena, Colombia, arrived for a visit: Jacobo, son of Uncle Maurice, and my cousin with his wife, a daughter, and a son. During the visit, I fell in love with Jacobo's daughter, so it was the occasion to send me to Colombia to live in a Jewish community and to complete my secondary education at the Hebrew School Union in Barranquilla.

The experience of living in an Israeli community and studying in a Jewish school (1975–1976) was significant for my personal development and reaffirmed my Jewish identity, as I actively participated in the Latin American Federation of Zionist Youth. They were also two generous years for exploring the gift of friendship, generosity, and solidarity once again. Life gave me very dear friends in those two years.

In the summer vacation of 1975, I traveled to France thanks to an airplane ticket that my sister Paulette, who worked for Iberia in Paris for 30 years, gave me. Getting to know the land where my father had been born, sharing with my sister Paulette, and knowing Paris, the city of light, entering Europe was a portal to the unknown, which filled me with excitement. Arriving at Charles de Gaulle airport was like arriving in the future. It had been opened a year before and was one of the icons of modernity. On the approximation to the Paris runway, I could see through the window the white vapor trails left by many planes. When we landed and taxied on the runway, I saw the Concorde transported on a platform. The Concorde was the only supersonic airplane (Match 2) for passengers that started flying in 1976. CHDG airport, with its futuristic architecture, elevated tunnels, and electric pathways of glass and aluminum, made me feel like I was in the future. We took the bus to the Arc de Triomphe (Etoile) and then a taxi to my sister's house in Belleville, in the 20th arrondissement (neighborhood), a middle-class neighborhood with a significant Jewish community that, since 1970, has become the place to resettle migrants from former French colonies in West Africa. It is now famous for the Père Lachaise cemetery, where my grandfather,

Yitshak, is buried, as well as famous people such as Jim Morrison (The Doors), Frederick Chopin, Honoré de Balzac, Marcel Proust, Édith Piaf, Molière, and Oscar Wilde, among others.

The time spent in Paris was fabulous. I was 17 years old with all the energy and curiosity about history and its leading figures. Paulette was a fan of museums and cultural presentations in the theater, movies, and opera, so I discovered the world of Art History with her. The Louvre, with its endless exhibit halls and famous Da Vinci's Mona Lisa, Rubens, Velázquez, and Rembrandt. The Impressionists in the Park of the Tuileries, with work done by major artists like Manet, Degas, Van Gogh, Renoir, and Cezanne. It was exciting to see the original works by Picasso, Dalí, and Miró, all of whom I had only heard about before.

I learned the story of that sad Paris from when my sister was little and had to hide from the Nazis who occupied the city and were looking for Jews to be taken to concentration camps. I walked around the streets of the Jewish neighborhood of Marais, witnesses of the hate and discrimination, and that now looked splendid with kosher food stores, bakeries, bookstores, a synagogue, and the Memorial Museum of Shoah (Holocaust). I visited the house where my father was born and lived at 44 Rue Charlot. I imagined what the city was like then (I imagined my grandfather Yitzhak with his horse and carriage selling fruit along those streets.)

I learned about the Paris of luxury and of living the good life of wealthy people at an apartment on the Champs-Élysées with an impressive view of the Eiffel Tower, where we were invited to dinner by friends of my sister's. But I also got to know the Paris of the beggars (clochards). One day, I felt hungry while visiting the Sanit Michelle neighborhood, the Latin Quarter, frequented by many young students. I decided to eat at a Vietnamese restaurant that caught my attention. While stepping inside, I noticed a man sitting on the sidewalk begging. I looked at him and felt compelled to invite him to have dinner with me. I helped him get up, and we went in together. To my surprise, he had excellent manners and seemed well educated. His name was Maxime; we had a pleasant conversation because he was very interested in learning about Colombia, Ecuador, and Latin America, a region he hadn't visited. When he learned about my interest in museums and the great Masters, he offered to accompany me to the Park of Tuileries, where the Impressionist exhibits were located at that time. I was amazed to discover that Maxime knew a great deal about the impressionists and guided me, providing incredible information about each one of the great masters and some of the most important works. When we returned to the park, I asked him why he knew so much about art, and he said he had learned since childhood, and later, while studying law, he had taken art courses. He had graduated as a lawyer from the Sorbonne. He later worked for an important Parisian law firm for many years, building a brilliant career. He had married and wanted to have a child. He was a happy man and made great efforts to achieve professional success and well-being for his family. Unfortunately, because he was so absorbed in his work, he didn't realize his wife was having an affair with another man. One day, he arrived home earlier than usual and found his wife in bed with another man. He told me, with tears in his eyes, that he couldn't react, that the surprise and pain from the betrayal were so great that he simply left without pronouncing a word. His world fell apart. Everything in which he believed, worked, and fought for ceased to be. His beliefs and values had been good for nothing; his dreams and passion for life had caused his blindness and absence from the reality of his marriage. So, he decided to abandon his career and material possessions and search for the idea of freedom, and that is why the streets of Paris had become his home and his world. He told me that by being a beggar, he had found liberty and time to be present in his life and thoughts. I was so young and full of ideas that this testimony from a friend who appeared out of nowhere moved me profoundly and made me appreciate him in a very special, compassionate, and, in some ways, very inspiring way. That afternoon, Maxime invited me to stay with him and witness his world to understand why he was happy now. I called my sister from a public telephone booth and told her I wouldn't be going home that night because a friend had invited me to spend the night at his home. I told her I would call her the next day to tell her how it had gone. We continued walking through the park, and later in the afternoon, we bought some sandwiches. When the night arrived, we went to sleep under the arch of a bridge across the Seine, where gigantic rats accompanied the beggars—underworld identities where hallucinations from alcoholism were part of everyday life.

Very early the following day, we went to a small place with coffee, milk, and a baguette with butter. Maxime took me to visit Victor Hugo's house museum in Vosges Plaza and to walk along old Paris; we ended the day in Montmartre, where we found many artists making a living by creating portraits of tourists with charcoal pencils. He had many friends who called him by his name. Maxime would approach them and talk with some of them. They laughed, and he would introduce me as his Latin American friend. As night approached, we got together with other homeless people in a dark corner, having a bonfire, wine, and laughs. Suddenly, there were hardly any people around; the vibrant bars and restaurants were closed, and the night's shadows and silhouettes transported me to a place of calm and serenity that I always remember and relate to those same spaces that have appeared in different parts of my life such as the mountains in El Cajas National Park in Cuenca, or the Amazon jungle where I spent so many years of my life. The following day, we had breakfast again and said goodbye. My sister wanted me to go to the Champagne Zone with some friends. When we said goodbye, I gave him my Levi jeans jacket. I asked for a photo, to which his answer was no because he preferred to be remembered just by memory, that he didn't want the memory to depend on a picture, and that his idea of freedom went that far. The truth is that I have always remembered and will remember Maxime. His memory will forever remain in my heart and mind. Maxime was the best gift on this unforgettable trip when I was 17.

I met Alex, a friend from the United States who lived with his grandparents in Paris. One night, we went snooping around the famous Place Pigalle in the red light district in Paris with sex shops, prostitution, striptease shows, and everything to do with sex culture. It was fascinating for me to see the world of sex in that dimension. Alex had been there many times and knew the best places to pry. The image that I most remember from that visit was that of Algerian immigrants forming a line in a secondary street at the doors to the prostitute's rooms, who offered their service for little money.

Alex called someone he knew and told her to invite one of her friends to go out with a South American friend who was visiting Paris. We met at the Park des Tuileries and had a fun day; we sunbathed with little clothing and finally agreed to go to Alex's grandparents' apartment because they had taken a four-day trip to their grandmother's sister's place in Toulouse. Alex was expecting his grandparents to arrive on the following day. We bought wine and celebrated a private party between the two couples. I found myself in the visitor's room with a beautiful blond French girl with blue eyes, naked in a charming encounter. Alex was in the same situation in his bedroom with his friend. Suddenly, we heard the door open. It was Alex's grandparents who had decided to return a day earlier. Panic, desperation, and shame all together. We dressed quickly, and while the grandparents reprimanded Alex, the three intruders ran out half-dressed. The girls and I ran to the metro station a few steps from the house; we had a nervous laugh attack and were in shock. We called Alex from a telephone booth to see how he was. The grandparents had been compassionate and did not make a big deal. Alex came out again, and we walked around Paris until dawn.

I met Jose Carlos, the son of my sister's Spanish colleague. He was a real character, a bit older than I, who got his livelihood by selling different objects that he got on the black market and placing them in shops in the big city. I explored the nightlife of Paris with him, Afro-French discos where people danced alone or in couples in front of a mirror that covered two walls of the dance floor. There were bars in cellars with live music and private parties. One day, we visited a salsa place called the Palace of the Lombardos near La Bastille. I didn't expect to find a salsa culture in Paris like any other tropical Latin American country. I felt at home with the music I carry within my pores, to dance...a beautiful brunette with braided curls and blue eyes crossed my path...Isabelle. We danced, drank, and fell in love, and at dawn, we ate onion soup in Les Halles. A great one-night love....

I crossed the English Channel by ferry to visit London. I stayed at a student residence in Kensington, very close to the Church of Saint Mary Abbots. I shared a dorm with six beds and a shared bathroom; 2 others shared the room. When I arrived, neither of the two was there. It was late, and I was tired and fell asleep. Yet, at dawn, I felt someone walking near my bed, so I opened my eyes. To my surprise, one of my roommates was walking around naked with a Charlie Chaplin hat and a closed umbrella, going over the union between the wall and the ceiling around the room. I didn't move and remained quiet, but scared. He walked around one more time and went to his bed. I requested a room change the next day.

The few days I spent in London were dedicated mainly to seeing the monuments and historical places and getting to know a bit of English culture. I enjoyed going to plays and theater concerts about the Beatles and Carol King, where I could only see a silhouette with lavish hair playing the piano live. Unforgettable!!

I returned to Paris and traveled to Spain by train a few days later. My intention was to arrive on time for the San Fermines in Pamplona. From now on, I wouldn't sleep in pensions or student residences; instead, I would use parks, fire stations, boats tied to the docks, and train stations. I carried a blanket, a pair of pants, three T-shirts, and two shirts in my backpack. I always had bulk wine, bread, and cheese, which were my sustenance in Spain 70% of the time. Pamplona had a carnival with troupes, street dances, groups of people drinking and singing in the streets, and a real party with people from all over the world. Bullfights and running of the bulls (bulls run through the city streets as part of the central tradition). We observed the first "encierro," or running of the bulls, to understand what it was all about. A pathway that goes from the municipality to the bullring was designed. They built a fence with wooden boards on the street, leaving a narrow corridor on the sidewalk between the wall and the houses. We saw our first encierro from a fixed point in a corner where we could see both streets.

We were ready for our bull race the next day. We went to the Municipality Plaza, where people gathered to start the race. We were all waiting for the firecracker signal. The majority of the people from Pamplona were dressed in white with a beret, a scarf around their necks, and a red sack on their waist, many of them holding a rolled-up newspaper in their hand, with which they started to hit their legs slowly and rhythmically. After the first firecracker, they started hitting their leg a little faster. As the second firecracker went off, people started jogging slowly as the cadence of the hits accelerated. When the third firecracker went off, the people started running, and soon after, the bulls appeared. The people ran wildly as the bulls ran past them. Then, more firecrackers were heard, a new group of bulls was announced, and the people started running desperately. When I saw the second group of bulls coming, I was terrified and tried to jump over the wooden fence. Still, the people there did not let me, and I had no option but to continue running in panic while the bulls kept passing by me. We arrived at the bullring, where a tunnel under the stands connected the exterior to the bullring. We ran into the tunnel to enter the ring, but to our surprise, people piled up against the tunnel's exit. It was as if there was a wall of bodies of the previous runners standing and piling up on purpose. Our only option was to climb over the bodies to make it to the ring and look for a wooden shield to make it to the arena's corridor and find a safe place to rest. The doors of the corrals were then opened, and friendly cows with bells came out. They calmed the bulls and guided them back to the corrals. Then several young bulls went out to the ring, and many of the runners went out to tease them without a cape, so you saw many people flying through the air, charged by the young bulls. I felt like a winner for running the whole circuit, but I thought about quitting at a certain point.

Behind the bullfighting ring was a small plaza with a statue of Ernest Hemingway, which I visited very excitedly because, during those days, I was reading his famous book "For Whom the Bell Tolls," which describes Pamplona and its surroundings during the Spanish Civil War.

After 5 days of San Fermines, I went to the famous Jazz festival of San Sebastian. Wonderful!! I wanted to be able to see Ella Fitzgerald live, who was the star of the festival that year. I remember a saxophone player was jamming; while playing the saxophone, he lay on the ground and moved, caressing the instrument as if it were a woman and passionately intimating. I was so touched that I let myself go with what the musician felt and had an euphoric experience that was so real that when the musician ended, I left to rest silently, far from the noise and the thousands of people around me.

One afternoon, I went to a beer bar packed with people, and there I met Toño, with long hair and a long black beard, dressed in black, who reminded me of Rasputin. We became friends and talked for a long while. Toño was very extroverted and became friends with a Spanish girl dressed as a hippy with an Indian blouse and a long, loose skirt with leather boots. Soon after, a friend of the girl arrived, and all four of us became friends. Then, Toño suggested we go with him to his country house outside San Sebastian. We bought some groceries, went to the train station, and traveled for about one hour until we reached a small train station surrounded by four houses. We walked for about an hour through the countryside and arrived at a hill with a cave whose entrance was covered in grapevines, which was Toño's country house. We lit candles because there was no electricity. The place was bare and straightforward. There were two beds, one on each extreme, an old wooden rectangular table, some chairs and stools, a hearth, and an easel to paint pictures with a table full of paints, paintbrushes, and canvases. Toño was a painter, and I found that out when we arrived at the cave. We spent four days and three unforgettable nights with music, sex, drugs, and art. We took long walks through the countryside, which was filled with abandoned houses due to the war between General Franco and the separatist group ETA. One night, until dawn, we heard distant rifle and machine gun fire. To bathe and collect water for cooking, we had to go down the hill to a small river with crystal-clear water surrounded by vegetation.

We returned to San Sebastian, and the jazz festival had already ended, so the city was calm and much less crowded. We said goodbye to our friends, and Toño asked me to wait for him at the beach, as he would see a friend to go to Bilbao together and visit his family. He took a while and then showed up with Iñaki, an old friend from elementary school. They arrived in a VW Safari convertible. I got on the rear, and we left for Bilbao. The road was parallel to the cliffs with wonderful forest and ocean views. We arrived in Bilbao and drove around the city, which looked dirty due to the soot on the walls of the buildings. The river was dirty, polluted, and had earth-colored water. We dropped Iñaki off at his house, then continued to Plentzia, where his parents lived, about half an hour away. I was surprised that Toño stopped the car before a Mansion's gate. He rang the bell, and the gate opened. We drove up to the house's porch through a big garden covered with grass and flowers, where an elegant lady with a grey suit and a bun appeared. Toño ran, saying mamaaaaa. He introduced me to her with a big hug, and I was welcomed. We went to Toño's room, where they gave us robes and asked us to wash all our clothing. We stunk. We had an excellent dinner with wine, coffee, and cookies on the porch at night to continue our chat.

Toño asked his parents for permission to sleep on the sailboat anchored in front of the house. After dinner, we rowed to the sailboat, where we spent the night resting under a refreshing breeze and in absolute peace.

The next day, I said goodbye to Toño and his parents, went to the train station, and bought a train ticket to Paris with my last money. A trip that lasted almost 12 hours. I shared my train space with

Portuguese workers returning to their jobs in Germany—kind people carrying abundant food that their wives had prepared for the trip. The cabin was inundated with smells and rumors whenever they decided to eat. They were always friendly and invited me to share their delicacies and company. Upon arrival in Paris, I even asked them for a couple of coins for the metro to return to my sister's house, which they gave me without any problem. Friendly people, good people....

I spent a few days with my sister before returning to Barranquilla, Colombia, to initiate my last year of High School.

It was also a time to experiment and live love in one of its most intense ways, with all the fervor and passion of youth. I visited Sarita, my girlfriend, every weekend in Cartagena for two years. She would become my wife and the mother of my three sons.

Graduation day arrived. My parents and sister came from Ecuador, and my family came from Cartagena. We participated in the solemn ceremony and the celebration offered at the High School. My father invited me to have a whisky with him for the first time. He was happy and loving as usual. He asked me, "And now, son, what have you thought? What do you want to do?"

"Well, Dad," I answered, "I would like to study biology at Michigan University." We carried out tests with my classmates, with the school's help, to learn about our abilities, possible careers, and contacts. I arrived at the University of Michigan as the best option for my University studies.

He told me that he would support me in any decision, but that it was vital for him to tell me that he felt he didn't have much time left, and that he was worried that something could happen to my mom and my sister, and the business with two hotels and about 36 employees. I asked him if he had been diagnosed with an illness or something, but he said no; he felt fine, but he knew he didn't have much time. This testimony from my father caused an intense moment of presence in that reality. I told him not to worry because we would go back home. We hugged each other and had another whiskey.

Parting with my girlfriend was emotional. We had been dating for two years, and she still needed to finish her last year of High School.

Back in Cuenca, I registered at the University of Azuay to study Business Administration and went back to live at my parents' house. My father gave me Hotel Cuenca while he managed Hotel Crespo. My mission was to learn how to manage a hotel by getting involved in all the operating areas, such as the kitchen and restaurant, housekeeping, front desk, public relations, marketing, and accounting.

Readapting to Cuenca after two years in Colombia and a first European trip was slow. But after the first year, which coincided with Sarita's graduation from High School, a feeling of wanting to be complete appeared. I was in love, so I talked to my parents about my desire to marry and start a family in Cuenca. My mother was happy and supported this option because she felt that it would give me stability and that I would settle down. Although my father adored Sarita, he worried we were too young and suggested we wait a bit. Between my mother's excitement and my love for Sarita, the wedding was evident. I went to Colombia to propose to Sarita and to ask for her hand in marriage. Her parents were happy about the consummation of our relationship. The wedding was to be carried out under the Jewish tradition, so I had to go through the conversion process because lineage is transmitted by the maternal line, and my mother was not Jewish. This was uncomfortable to me because to legitimize my identity, feelings, and will, I had to go through a forced process.

Nevertheless, I did it with much effort and dedication to satisfy and normalize the circumstances in the family and social context. Studying Jewish culture and history during the two years I attended the Colegio Hebreo Union in Barranquilla was very helpful. As well as my activism in the Movement for Latin American Zionist Youth. Still, I had to study religious and ceremonial topics. Although my father was never a practicing Jew and was married to a non-Jewish woman, he had kept the Covenant. He had me circumcised on the 8th day after my birth in Quito by the Mohel of the Jewish community of that time. I stood before a Rabi council for three consecutive days. I was questioned about different aspects of history, culture, and religion. I went through a physical examination. We talked about personal and family motivations and about the reasons for being. I was converted.

I could marry under the Jewish tradition, complying with the Ketubah (Jewish marriage contract).

We married in Cartagena with a traditional Jewish ceremony with family and friends. We went to Mexico for our honeymoon. We visited Mexico City and flew to Acapulco. When we took our seats on the plane, the plane took off, and I picked up the offered newspaper. I read the news that an airplane from San Airlines had had an accident in Ecuador while flying between Quito and Cuenca. Among the crew's names was my Aunt Martha Carrera, my mother's sister, who worked as a stewardess and lived with us in Cuenca. A great pain just starting the honeymoon....

After our honeymoon in Acapulco, we enjoyed the classic visits to bars and restaurants. On the morning of the 4th day, and after having partied the night before, I got up early and went to the bank. I left Sarita placidly sleeping. The bank was about three blocks from the hotel. I went in to change $300 in traveler's checks. I was returning to the hotel when I noticed a VW Beetle parked near me and the driver signaling me to approach the car. When I was by the door on the driver's side, I felt a knife in my back and two men insulting me and ordering me to get in the car. The driver had opened the door. They forced me into the back by hitting me with extreme coarseness. They drove to an inhabited zone for about half an hour outside of Acapulco. They parked the car out of the road and pushed me out. Out of the three thieves, there was one who was very violent. He smashed the beer bottle he was drinking and threatened to hurt me with the broken rim.

The other thief tried to calm him and wanted me to give him the money. They picked my pockets and stole a pair of Ray-Ban glasses and a pair of black leather clogs, the only shoes I had for the honeymoon. Then, they would ask me who I was with and the name of my hotel. I kept telling them that I was with a group of friends and gave them the name of another hotel. They continued with this psychological game by terrifying, offending, and denigrating me. There were moments when I was so furious that I wanted to attack them. I kept imagining how I would do it. Still, the possibility of failing would appear, and then I would probably be killed and thrown in that place, and I would never be found. And Sarita was on honeymoon, sleeping in our hotel. That image prevented me from acting, and I allowed them to continue offending me. Finally, when they saw that I was a wreck, they made fun of me and left me in that unknown place without shoes and morally destroyed. I walked on my bare feet for a while on a gravel road; my feet were bleeding, the sun was hitting hard, and I was crying out of anger. I had been humiliated to the extreme, as never in my life. I had never experienced that degree of humiliation, frustration, and impotence. After a long time, I reached a paved road with traffic, where I stopped a taxi and asked to be taken to the hotel. I told the taxi driver what had happened and asked him to wait at the entrance until I got some money from the reception desk to pay for his service. When the people at the desk saw me, sweaty, crying, and with bleeding feet, they took care of the taxi driver. I went up to the room and took two steps inside. When I saw Sarita placidly sleeping and smelled the aromas of our clothes and bodies, I kneeled on the floor and started crying inconsolably. The next day, without shoes—as I said, the clogs were the only shoes I had brought to the honeymoon, and I found it impossible to find my size (Size 13) in the hotel zone—I had to go barefoot to the old city to find shoes my size. Finally, I found some old models for gringos that I happily bought for a decent return.

We returned to Mexico City, rented a car, and drove around the central part of the country. We left for San Miguel Allende, a beautiful little town with white houses with geraniums on their windows and narrow streets. Mario Moreno Cantinflas and Pedro Vargas had their summer houses in this town. My wife was wandering around in a Mexican arts and crafts shop. The owner was an older German man, a refugee from WWII, with whom I started a conversation. When he found out I was from Ecuador, he started talking about Latin American Indigenous people with feelings of disdain, saying things like the only thing you can do with them is to feed them and make them work because they are lazy. I got upset and told him they needed education, respect, and opportunities, and to pay them fair salaries. The shop owner insisted on his position, which upset me, so I went outside.

A very kind man approached me. He was plump and tall. He had a beard and was a bit bald. He was wearing a Levi's shirt. He told me he had heard my discussion with the shop owner and that he was pleased with what I had said; he was probably a Nazi. We started conversing, and I told him I was on my honeymoon with my wife. He suddenly invited me to spend the weekend at his house, where he would meet friends coming from Guanajuato and Mexico City. A bit surprised by this unexpected invitation, I told my wife. We doubted for a moment, but felt good about it and accepted it. Since we were on our way to Queretaro, it was easy for us to change plans, and it was only for one night.

Pablo had an excellent Jeep with a leather hood. He asked us to follow him through a stony road surrounded by vegetation. We drove further, and I started to get nervous because the place looked desolate. It was very far before we suddenly arrived at a big wooden gate under a stone arch covered by ivy. When we went in, we were surprised to find a beautiful mansion built with wood, stone, and glass surrounded by exuberant vegetation. It was a spectacular house with extensive areas and a great outside terrace that faced a gorge with a gigantic waterfall. I had only seen this in movies. They gave us a beautiful room with a fantastic view of the waterfall. They let us rest and invited us to the appetizers at the end of the afternoon.

We appeared at the soiree and met the six other guests who had arrived from different parts. It was an interesting group of people, including academics, journalists, social activists, and artists. Among the artists was one of the most important classical guitarists from

Mexico, who played the ¨Concierto de Aranjuez¨ masterfully. The conversations revolved around organizing the political and social scenarios now that they would be legally recognized. They were members of the Mexican communist party operating in clandestinity then. It was a fleeting experience that showed me the faces of idealists who were convinced of their dreams and their presence in political activism, which presented itself in a totally random manner.

The following day, we shared a calm, fresh breakfast on the terrace with the guests, and later we each went our own way. Thank you, San Miguel de Allende. Thank you, Pablo.

I started my new married life in Cuenca. We found a good place near my parents. I continued my university studies in business administration and managed Hotel Cuenca. Learning with my father was a profoundly delightful experience because of his patience and natural way of doing things, mainly because of the respect and love I perceived all the employees, providers, and clients had for him. The cooking practices were intense since we did them through catering and à la carte restaurant services. He also made me study the book Larousse Gastronomique, which always accompanied him to his office. I learned that one of the strengths that he insisted on was his personal attention as a host, making his clients feel an individual and particular relationship and service. This has become one of my personal strengths with time.

5. My Father's Death

I was a member of Estudiantes Club, a semi-professional soccer club. I was the goalkeeper, and we practiced daily on the University of Cuenca's soccer field. On July 2, 1979, I returned to my parents' house for lunch after training. When I arrived, I noticed many cars and people. I remember that Carlos, one of the hotel employees, was standing on the balcony with a somber face, which indicated that something terrible had happened. I ran in and found out that my father had died while he was napping after lunch. I went up to his room, and he was there, lying dead on his bed, with his eyes closed. I could not believe it. I hugged him, asking him to wake up, kissing and caressing his head with a feeling of desperation, anguish, fear, and total desolation. At that moment, I realized that death couldn't be the end of everything and that there was nothing more. That idea was not possible with my father, so since then, I have believed in the soul and its transcendence after death.

That day at noon, we had been together at Hotel Crespo, looking at his white Mercedes-Benz. He knelt on the floor to try to see underneath the car because something was making a sound. I helped him and told him that there was nothing loose and that later on at home, we could look into it better. As usual, I kissed his cheek goodbye, saying I was attending training and would see him later.

It was as if the floor had been taken away from under my feet, and I recalled what my father had said at my graduation three years before—that he didn't have much time left, and that was how it was. From a different perspective, I understood how lucky I had been to have a man like him as my father and to receive so many life examples about love, loyalty, integrity, effort, and conscious and voluntary sacrifice.

My life changed radically from that day. I was 21 years old, in charge of 2 hotels, and responsible for my mother and sister, just as my father said on my graduation. It became the most significant challenge of my life to comply with my father's expectations and feel the great responsibility I had to assume. Initially, it was tough because many of the Hotel workers who had been there a long time and had known me since childhood could not process the fact that I was now their boss. The other problem was the providers who took away my credit. I was forced to pay for everything in cash: the chicken, shrimp and seafood, meat, alcoholic and non-alcoholic beverages, cleaning products, and others. This affected the cash flow and supplies.

One day, less than a year after my father's death, a friend of my dad's, Doctor Flores, came to see me. He was opening a new building for the General Comptroller's office in Cuenca. He wanted me to be in charge of the opening banquet, attended by many authorities, presidents of different groups, and special guests from Quito and Guayaquil. It was the best opportunity to demonstrate that Hotel Crespo remained the city's best catering option. I gathered all the personnel and told them that we would be preparing a banquet for 300 of the most influential people in the city and that it would be the most incredible opportunity to demonstrate the work legacy we inherited from Don Henry. My mother also supported me with her presence. She motivated the personnel, who were totally devoted to her, to put their heart and soul into their work.

The buffet we presented was impressive. It had a decorated one-meter-long bass accompanied by steamed lobsters, sirloin with mushrooms and demi-glace, Vizcaine calamari, whiskey shrimp, chicken rolls with spinach filling, and assorted vegetables. The table was decorated with pink arupo flowers and lighted from below with fluorescent lights. There was a cheese table, a dessert table, and a fantastic brigade of chefs and servers to offer excellent service. It was wonderful. All the guests appreciated the beauty, the quality of the food, and the service. I was there throughout the reception because the guests needed to see me directing to reestablish confidence in the business, which was now under my command.

That same night, I received multiple congratulations from a significant number of people who knew my father and who were pleased to see that the personnel and I were honoring his memory and his legacy; during the following weeks, we had a significant number of reservations and contracts for catering services for weddings and christenings. Important companies in the area, such as Artepráctico, Zhumir, Empresa Eléctrica, and Desarrollo Agropecuario, requested our services. Success and committed work allowed us to endure the business and comply with all our obligations and needs.

One day, a good lawyer friend visited me at Hotel Cuenca and asked for a favor. He asked me if I could hide in the hotel an ex-leader of the Shuar Indigenous nationality, Ernesto Tserem (ET), who had been vice-president of the Shuar Federation and who at the moment had been accused of murder. Eduardo had been helping him voluntarily for two years because the police were looking for him in the country. He needed to be near the Superior Court of Justice in Cuenca, which had jurisdiction over Morona Santiago province. Eduardo said that the trial was about to end and that many documents had to be signed when needed.

ET stayed at my hotel for about 7 months, and we developed a strong, close friendship. One night, we were drinking rum in his room, and stimulated by the sweetness of the alcohol, I shared a sorrow that I had of not being able to have children. I knew that I was the cause of the problem because we had already done all the possible exams and treatments with my wife. ET comforted me and told me not to worry; he was going to talk to his two wives, who were sisters, and ask them to bring his father-in-law, Don Ambrosio, who was a shaman, to help me. Fifteen days later, his two wives and their father visited ET and met the lawyer and friend helping him. They spent a week in Cuenca, during which time I stayed at the hotel and took them around Cuenca and nearby places. It was the first time that the ladies and the Shaman were visiting a big city because they had only been to Macas and Sucua. When we said farewell, Ambrosio asked ET to translate that he would return soon with medicine to help me.

About a month later, he arrived with one of the daughters and the medicine he had brought from the jungle. A powder made from the dissected penis of a nocturnal marsupial, a compound of sun-dried medicinal herbs, a tree bark for infusions, and Natem, known to the Western world as Ayahuasca.

He asked me to fast one day from morning until dusk when he would have a healing ceremony. The appropriate place to carry it out was my house, so I called my friend Juan Maldonado and his wife, Yoya, to come over and be with Sarita and to take care of me in case of a strange episode. We prepared the living room, and I lit the fireplace to make it more appropriate. ET, his father-in-law, and one of his wives arrived. The first thing Don Ambrosio asked was to put out the fire and turn off all the lights in the house, which surprised me. Still, he explained that total darkness was necessary for the ceremony. It was my first experience with Ayahuasca. He served the medicine for him, first, then for me, and then for ET to cleanse him from the paranoia he had lived with during the last 2 years.

After about 45 minutes, the medicine started to take effect. I felt a sharp pain in my stomach, a mixture of cramps, twists, gags, and then intense dizziness. These uncomfortable symptoms lasted for a while, and then I started to see geometrical figures in fluorescent colors that passed before me. They would appear and disappear, then give way to other intense visions. Throughout my hallucinations, Don Ambrosio's singing and whistling accompanied me without interruption. In a moment, he stopped whistling, and I felt his mouth on my lower belly, where he started to suck forcefully and intensely in the area around my belly button. It took forever, and sometime during the procedure, I felt as if the sucking sensation took my whole body; I felt that Don Ambrosio was sucking me from my head to my toes. I fell profoundly asleep. The next day, I found out through my guests that he had worked for a long time, but only in the lower belly zone. When I woke up early the following day, he gave me a medicinal herb tea with a powder he had prepared. I took that combination for the next 7 days.

Don Ambrosio stayed with me the whole day, and at night, he returned to Sucua on a bus with his daughter. A little while later, Eduardo won the trial for ET, who was declared innocent of the crime he was accused of. Everyone in his community near Palora knew the story of ET, so when news of his freedom arrived, they got ready for his reception. ET invited Eduardo and me to go with him to his community, where he had been absent for over 2 years. We arrived in

Palora and walked for another hour and a half through pastures, orchards, and jungle.

When we arrived at the community, everyone awaited their mate, the ex-vice President of the Shuar Federation of Ecuador. It was a great reception, demonstrating appreciation and happiness for ET's declaration of innocence.

The atmosphere and the people with feathered crowns on their heads and faces decorated in red Achiote and black paint impressed us. After the required words, the community's Official representative gave an official welcome, and then ET and one of the community's elders offered food. There was a table for a group of people, authorities from neighboring communities, teachers, and guests, and another smaller table where ET, the Shaman, and a few elders were seated. ET was allowed to drink chicha and eat some plantain and cassava.

ET fasted the whole next day at the healer's house. At the same time, we participated in a community fishing activity with the families in a small river, a 1-hour walking distance from the town. We washed a long root called barbasco, which had previously been crushed, placed it in baskets (chankinas), and took it to the river. The baskets were then submerged in the little river with the crushed root, and a white substance came out and was diluted in the river. About 70 meters downriver, many people participating in the fishing collected the fish that had floated down due to the lack of oxygen in the water, where the root was diluted, which chemically consumed the oxygen in the water. There were abundant fish of all sizes collected without waiting, not even the tiny fish. Another 50 meters downriver, a group weaved a particular net with lianas and sticks, which conducted the fish towards a funnel where any fish that had not been caught in the previous parts ended up.

Another group, a few men, many women, and children, was making several fires on the riverbanks where the fish were collected. Most of the catch was steamed on wooden grills over the fire. Another group hung the baskets (chankinas) high above the fires to smoke on the higher part. It carried them back to the communal kitchen. There were also other pots with plantain and yucca, and others were making fish soup with the bones and heads of the bigger fish. All of these were under the trees on the river banks. It was a time to make and share with everyone who had a common interest. When it was time to eat, everyone gathered around the fire, and chicha was served along with the food, and then again, the chicha. There was great humor, jokes, and laughs for a long time until it was time to gather all the catch, fill baskets and backpacks made by the river with lianas and palm leaves, and return to the community.

The next day, ET, a shaman, and one of the elders went to the waterfall. We silently accompanied them for about an hour until we arrived at the shore of a small river. They crossed the river and disappeared into the forest. The waterfall where they had the purification ceremony for ET with Malikoa-Guanto (Datura arborea,

Solanaceae) was about 30 minutes from the small river. They remained by the waterfall for two nights; they returned to the community on the morning of the third day. ET had an expressionless face, as if he were looking into the void; he was looking at us but did not see us. They took him home so he could sleep while inhaling tobacco through his nose to give him a good rest.

ET showed up the next day for lunch. He greeted us and looked again like he used to be. According to his tradition, we didn't comment or ask anything about his purification. The only thing he said was that he received his power once again and that he felt calm. After lunch, Eduardo and I left for Macas, and the next day, after 10 hours, we arrived in Cuenca.

This experience was something extraordinary at this moment in my life. I had been working and studying for 4 years, I had been married for 3 years, and I had been doing treks in the Cajas National Park for condor-watching with those guests from Hotel Cuenca and Hotel Crespo, enjoying this activity with people who wanted a little adventure. We would do 1, 2, and 3-day excursions to the Cajas. My local friends helped me. These friends used remote areas of El Cajas as pastures for their wild cattle. Don Oswaldo, Homero, and Froilan knew the area and contributed with horses, mules, guiding, and logistics. We formed a beautiful team. The Andean paramo was a kingdom of silence where you could only hear your breathing and the wind.

I wanted to explore the Amazon and its people to develop an alternative tourism program. Its most significant expressions are the beauty and power of nature in the jungle, the sophisticated knowledge of the humans who inhabit it to survive in such demanding conditions, the rituals of daily life, and total self-sufficiency.

The Palora area wasn't adequate because of cattle and tea plantations, which were beginning to expand. I visited the Shuar Federation of Ecuador in Sucua, the Indigenous organization of which ET had been vice president. The trip from Cuenca to Sucua via Limon Indanza was spectacular due to the geography of the Western Cordillera of the Andean paramo. It passed through cloudy forests until the lowlands at 1000 meters above sea level, where Macas and Sucua are found. These are cities of the Ecuadorian Amazon and the last urban settlements before the Amazon rainforest.

The visit to the Shuar Federation was essential in understanding the degree of organization and work of the Shuar people/Nation. They had a parliamentary-type organization with leaders elected by popular vote in assemblies, with representatives of all the Shuar communities of the Shuar nation present in our territory. They alternated every three years. Their principal site had a complex infrastructure with offices for the President, vice president, treasurer, and each leader in the health area, who monitored some health centers and health promoters. They had education through a system of Bicultural Bilingual Education, with tutorials aired on radio stations and teachers in situ in the communities. Territory, Organizational empowerment, and Communication through their own short-wave radio station with a regular service of news, communications, and school classes. They also had a central HF radio with an operator who made daily broadcasts in the morning and afternoon, where most communities connected. In Sucua, they had an interpretation and formation center, a small museum, a zoo with Amazonian species, and a crafts shop where they sold crafts made by women from different communities. There was a section of books from the Mundo Shuar series, published by Salesians under the Don Bosco/Abya Yala editorials, featuring many works by missionaries, anthropologists, and sociologists who had explored and studied the Shuar culture. I found some fabulous academic books and a collection of myths and ceremonies there. This information fed my fantasy about this place's mysteries and people. It awakened an immense curiosity and a strong calling to discover this world.

The interprovincial Federation of Shuar-Achuar centers emerged in 1964 when Ecuador initiated agricultural reform, and a law to colonize the Amazonian region was contemplated. This law could put the integrity of ancestral Indigenous territories of the people of the Amazon at risk. The Roman Catholic religious congregations of the Salesians, disciples of Saint John Bosco, who assist, accompany, and finance their Mission of the Vicariate of Mendez, the Shuar in implementing the Shuar Federation. The Salesian mission has one of its principal places in Macas, where they operated the Missionary Air

Services (SAM in Spanish), which was one of the few air services in the Amazonian region then together with Alas del Socorro belonging to the North American Evangelical Mission based in Shell in the Pastaza province and a small plane belonging to CREA (Center for Economic reconversion of Azuay, Cañar and Morona Santiago) a state office for the development of this southern region of the country.

When I visited the Missionary Air Service to find out how to access flights to the jungle, I met the Head Pilot, Captain Jose Arcos. He told me about his father, a secular missionary, Don Juan Arcos, who managed a mission beyond the Cutucú Cordillera called Miazal. Don Juan had received groups of German students for 4 years, brought by Professor of Biological Sciences Erwin Ptzet, a scientific eminence who lived in Ecuador for many years and was the author of the book Flora and Fauna of Ecuador.

After visiting the Salesian bishop in Macas to present my intention of developing cultural tour groups with benefits for the communities, I got his authorization, which allowed me to access the SAM flights. I then met Father Adriano Barale, Salesian in charge of the direction and administration of the Missionary Air Service, who knew the Shuar and Achuar communities of the zone very well and, upon seeing my intentions, was generous enough to give me the green light over the viable possibilities. He was always my important reference and friend during the 12 years I flew in that zone.

Daniel Koupermann C.

5-5

5-6

List of photos

Photos of the Origin:

1. Henry and Yoly at 24 years old

2. Henry, first on the left

3. The three brothers: Henry (soldier), Gregorio (businessman), and Ramón (firefighter)

4. Henry with Juan X Marcos' German pilot, Salinas, 1946

5. Henry, on the left

6. Henry and Yoly, joyful together

7. The Koupermann–Malherbe family; Father at 6–7 years old, France

8. My mother, Yoly, at 22 years old

9. Grandmothers Anna and Marina

10. Father, Mother, and Danny at age two, on the swing

11. Family with sister Paulette

12. Danny with Father

13. Grandparents Yitzhak and Anna upon arriving in France from Russia

14. My sister Giselle and her family

15. Danny at 10 months with Paulette, Uyumbicho

16. With my granddaughter Josy

6. Shuar—Miazal

In 1981, I flew to Miazal to meet Don Juan Arcos, learn about the place, and evaluate the possibility of taking visitor groups. The small plane, a Helio Courier, took off, and when we were above the Cutucu Cordillera with its virgin, unexplored rain forests, the hills and valleys, and the exuberant vegetation, I was opened up to a fascinating world.

We arrived at Miazal, where Don Juan Arcos awaited us at the airstrip. The airstrip was located on the shores of the Mangosiza River. We took a canoe and, with a lever, navigated downriver for about 35 minutes to the mouth of the Tsuirim River, which we took for another 30 minutes until we arrived at the camp house, where we disembarked and where Doña Amalia, a Shuar woman, the wife of Don Juan, was waiting for us.

Doña Amalia was a woman of power and was very well respected by the Shuar people. She was Don Juan's support as a secular missionary in managing the Mission of Miazal, where 120 students from first to 12th grade were educated.

They were my first teachers about the jungle people and the jungle itself.

Don Juanito was totally dedicated to the Mission. He directed all the daily operations. He was in charge of daily morning prayers when

Father Raul, a Salesian missionary, was not around. He also managed and coordinated with the teachers, as the Mission was primarily an educational center where students from surrounding homes and communities studied. It was also an internship with around 70 boys and girls who, apart from education, were also in charge of carrying out work to sustain life in the Mission. Don Juan had a profound knowledge of the Shuar way of thinking after living amongst them for many years and marrying a Shuar woman. He had a natural empathy with that culture and was part of it. He was a great storyteller who knew the family and social relations of many of the Shuar of Mangosiza, Morona, Kangaime, and Macuma rivers. He initially oriented me on what to do and how to do things.

Doña Amalia was knowledgeable about the jungle's secrets, medicinal plants, animals, ceremonies, and spiritual world. She was my great teacher for 12 years. I am so grateful for everything I received from her. Additionally, we shared many nights cooking together for groups. When you cook with someone, a great intimate conversation space is opened. She was a dear friend and teacher.

Doña Amalia was my companion on my first exploration of the thermal waterfall upriver on the Tsuirim River (Hot water). This is one of the most beautiful and impressive treks of the Amazon jungle that I have seen. We followed the river's course from the valley where the Mission lay towards the Cutucú Cordillera, where the riverbed became so narrow that the only access was through the river itself with gigantic rocks, rapids, and pools. At one point, we had to walk with water up to our chests and the backpacks on our shoulders. After 3 hours, we finally arrived at a haven in the river canyon. There sprang from the rock a 6-meter-high hot waterfall on the right bank. It was hot enough that it generated vapor clouds. Five meters away, another waterfall with great volume fell directly onto the river haven. There were gigantic trees on both sides of the cliffs of this paradise. To arrive there with Doña Amalia and witness the profound respect she showed the place, which for her represented the sublimity of nature. It was a sacred space. She said, "Let's ask for permission, and thanks for the power of being here."

I took travelers to this place for 12 years, averaging 6 to 8 groups yearly. This trek was always one of the most appreciated activities because of the experience it offered, the tremendous physical effort, and the overwhelming natural beauty.

After my previous experience with Ayahuasca in Cuenca, I was interested in the possibility of doing ceremonies. I told Doña Amalia, and when she understood where my interest came from, she explained and told me so many stories about powerful medicinal plants (Datura, Ayahuasca, Tobacco), the differences among them, and the meaning for the jungle people who use them. She shared her experiences taking the medicine at times and serving it at other times, especially to her children, so they would have vision in their lives. Of course, to be able to access that information from a Shuar matron opened up, once again, a fascinating aspect of the inhabitants of that wonderful world.

I asked Doña Amalia how we could know if we could do ceremonies. She told me she would like to take me to the big waterfall with a Uwichin (Shaman) and have the ceremony there. She sent a message to Elder Chumpi's house, which was two hours away, asking him to come with us. The following day, towards the end of the afternoon, Chumpi arrived with his wife and teenage son at the house camp. They stayed with us, and we dined and socialized with Chumpi, who did not speak Spanish; the communication was through his son and Doña Amalia.

We left the next day for the big waterfall; it took 5 hours to climb up the foothills of the Cutucu Cordillera. After climbing for 3 hours, we went down the ravine to where the waterfall lay. We descended with ropes until we reached a small flatland where Doña Amalia indicated we should leave the tents and supplies. We continued on our way down for about 15 minutes, where we found a small river, and walked for 10 more minutes upriver, where we arrived at a great hollow in the middle of the forest with a 70 to 80-foot-tall waterfall. Spectacular!! The waterfall formed a great pool at its base, allowing you to walk to the water jet. The hurricane wind that the fall caused in the hollow was impressive; it moved water spray in its fall, together with the sound it made, creating a unique space. For the Amazonians, waterfalls are sacred places where the spirit of Arutam (God) manifests itself; they are like holy temples, portals for the great spirit.

I felt like I was in a temple, holy ground, creation manifested at its most extraordinary splendor. The physical effort of the trek and the fasting helped me focus on my purpose: requesting permission to explore the place and to know whether I could bring groups of foreigners to experiment with what I was living at that moment.

Elder Chumpi greeted the waterfall, asked for permission while singing his Icaro, and asked us to introduce ourselves by whispering our name and last name and communicating our intention. I thanked the moment and the opportunity, asking for protection, illumination, and anything else the medicine would offer. I had Doña Amalia's advice for the Natem (Ayahuasca) to manifest and accompany me, giving me clarity:

1. Do not be afraid, no matter what you see or feel in the vision.
2. Yield, give yourself up, do not control, and do not let your thoughts have space in your experience; it is a moment to be your intimate self.
3. Keep your intention present and be thankful.

We stood in the internal space and silence before the waterfall for a long time. Then, we returned to where we had set up our camp.

As night approached, we formed a circle; Chumpi served the medicine (NATEM-AYAHUASCA: Banisteriopsis caapi, cooked with CHACRUNA: *Psychotria viridis*). The first serving was for him, and the Uwishins always drank it first to awaken their power and the power of the medicine. To be able to 'see,' they need to drink. He served the dose in a little bowl, put it to his mouth, concentrated, and started to whistle and sing his Icaro. Each Shaman has his own Icaro, sings, whistles, blows alternatively on the medicine to awaken it, and then drinks. Each of the participants at the ceremony carried out this exact procedure.

After we all drank, we remained together for a moment while Chumpi continued to sing. When he was silent, we each searched for a place to rest comfortably, wrap up, and wait for the medicine to manifest itself. That moment was so unique that I felt moved and willing to surrender and be present with happiness and humility. My feelings slowly became sharper: color, geometric figures paraded, very pretty, the canopy's silhouettes against the starry sky in the back, the sound of the water in the waterfall, the insects, bats, and other sounds, all synchronized into a beautiful symphony.

A moment of physical discomfort when I felt stomach cramps, some vomit, and gags with very acute diaphragm contractions, but with the idea of giving up, surrendering without fear, or controlling those unpleasant moments. The visions continued with the waterfall, the jungle, rivers, lagoons, and native peoples with painted faces, recreating the myth of Natem, in which the sun Etsa, the great warrior, virtuous hunter, leader, and father, lived with the humans. It was like paradise because He was always there to help solve human problems, until one day humans stopped being consequential, offending Him gravely. Etsa divided the heavens and left a climbing liana (Natem) as a medium for ascending, connecting with Him, and receiving his advice and help.

Etsa sent Ayumpum, a warrior, in the form of lightning to the Earth, where he adopted a human form and taught the humans to prepare the liana, the NATEM (Ayahuasca) medicine. The image of Ayumpum I had seen in the Mission's chapel was of a warrior adorned with feathers and seeds with a spear, cooking the head of a living jaguar in a large clay pot. This image was present in my vision that night, blending with other visions for a long time. Dawn arrived, and we got up in silence. I felt complete, happy, and relieved to have had such meaningful visions; the Amazon rainforest, its people, and its animals manifested themselves with maximum splendor.

We went to the waterfall to cleanse ourselves under the diffused water jets. I rendered my thanks. I was touched, remembering the previous afternoon when we saw the waterfall for the first time, and I approached it to introduce myself and request permission. I felt that the waterfall embraced and accepted me.

Going back to this experience, I understand why I have spent 40 years facilitating travelers' encounters with the ancestral knowledge of Indigenous peoples and the natural beauty of the Amazon rainforest.

We returned to the camp house next to the Miazal Mission to rest and process our unforgettable experience.

The Miazal Mission was the home of Father Raul de Vriess, a Salesian priest from Belgium who had already lived many years in the jungle with the Shuar. He was a missionary and a trekker who offered the word and healed people. He was a wonderful character. The missionary work he carried out blended with the Shuar way of life. The Shuar called him ETSA (Sun), which, according to the Shuar mythology, represents the virtuous and wise man, the excellent hunter, fisherman, warrior, best friend, father, and husband.

Father Raul lived in a little indigenous hut about 300 meters from the Mission. The only difference from a Shuar hut was a plastic roof to let in light, book stands, and a table with three chairs. He shared his time at home with six hens, all with proper women's names. They were his allies in his Mission to heal gravely ill patients who went to see him. His magical recipe for these patients included chicken broth, vitamins and minerals, patience, and love. I could testify during my frequent visits to the Mission how the father healed a man who had been declared terminally ill in the Cuenca Hospital.

Whenever I arrived with groups at Miazal, I always brought chocolates for Father Raul, aware of how much he enjoyed them. When I went to his house to give him the chocolates and greet him, there was always time for a conversation. He would talk to his hens and explain who the patient to be healed was. He requested their help and asked for forgiveness for the sacrifice they had to go through to offer chicken broth for the sick. It was a magical world, but so real... it seemed the hens understood and helped him.

The Mission's kitchen always had a clay pot with Father Raul's chicha, which was always very strong and fermented. He had his daily meals at the Mission with the students, and that was also where the chicken broth for the ill was prepared. A holy man!

I kept carrying foreign traveler groups uninterrupted to Miazal for 12 years. Initially, Suiss from Intertrek, an agency belonging to a dear friend, Margarita Niedermaier, spent many years with eight groups per year, with whom we spent 6 days in the Amazon, combined with a 2-week cruise in the Galapagos. Margarita only offered 15-day cruises to the islands. They were exceptional clients focused on learning about nature, enjoying it thoroughly, and receiving quality information about the human and natural history of the Amazon region. I also remember, with affection, Irma Turtle of Turtle Tours in Colorado, USA. We used to carry out combined Mazan Forest-Cajas National Park itineraries with Miazal and shamanic visits to Illuman and Aguarongo in Imbabura.

It was a time of much learning, and where I formed the basis to become a naturalist expedition leader for the rest of my life.

After around 3 years of operating in Miazal, I bought a 6-meter-long aluminum boat and started to make longer trips. I started with 4 days in Miazal, and then we navigated downriver to the Mangosiza River. We rode the Morona, Cangaime, Macuma, and Wichimi rivers until we arrived at the Achuar community of Wichimi after 6 days of traveling. For me, two stops were a life school and, for the travelers, an essential part of the jungle experience. The visit to Elder Tukupi on the Cangaime river and to the Achuar community in Wichimi, where I made dear friends, including Wakiash, one of the community leaders; Elder Mukuimbiu; his son Tsamaren; Ramu and his two wives, among others.

Elder Tukupi was one of the last Shuar warriors who had participated in wars against the Achuar and other Shuar groups. He said he had a few hidden shrunken heads (Tzantzas) of his enemies from the clan wars. The Shuar are the only Jibaro group (Achuar, Huambisas, Aguarunas, Shuar) who used to shrink their enemy's heads. They are not war trophies but rather the only possible protection so that the vengeful spirit of the victim will not bother or threaten the victimizer. They are very well hidden to ensure protection. Nevertheless, the family of the victim will have an obligation to avenge the death through war or by killing the victimizer who has a shrunken head. A vicious circle of revenge was established through wars and/or killings.

There was a traditional coming-of-age ceremony for young men. They had to go alone to the jungle, hunt a sloth, and shrink its head. Apart from demonstrating their abilities as hunters at finding jungle animals, they learned how to reduce heads with hot stones and sand, cold water, and anticoagulant plants. It is a complex process that lasts for some weeks. You must dedicate yourself fully and without interruptions to ensure the reduction is produced correctly. These days, this activity is illegal and punishable by law.

Elder Tukupi and I built an extraordinary and close friendship. His knowledge of the jungle, the plants, and the animals, and his interpretation of natural phenomena became a source of knowledge and inspiration for me. I learned so much from him and have beautiful memories of our time together. We shared treks from his home to a lake 2 hours away from his house. On the way, he was always attentive to finding animals, so he walked stealthily, and we all followed him in the same way. He used to find serpents on the trees, Jaguar and Tapir tracks, and tracks from other animals such as deer, guatusas, dantas, and guantas. He was like an encyclopedia. Once, I had Scottish passengers: Gowan, the father, and his son Logan, who recently graduated from high school. His father had promised a once-in-a-lifetime adventure trip that he would never forget as a graduation gift. The trip included the Amazon jungle and a bear-hunting trip in Alaska.

After trekking in Miazal, we visited Elder Tukupi to carry out nocturnal fishing in a lake, where we arrived on wooden canoes rowing upriver on the Caigaime River. Once at the lagoon, we used 3 three canoes: A big one with Gowen and Logan, Marcelino, the Shuar guide, and me; a small canoe with Elder Tukupi and one of his sons; another small canoe with my friend Juan Vaca and Carlos Arcos, my traveling companion, Don Juan, and Doña Amalia's son.

It was a clear night with a waxing moon, and the three canoes were 30 meters and 100 feet apart. They all had fish hooks. Suddenly, something bit Logan's bait, but it offered no resistance; it was as if the fishhook had gotten stuck. Logan asked me what to do, and I took the fishing line in my hand and felt a pull, as if there were a dead weight. I suddenly felt a big pull that hit my arm abruptly, and it started to move. You could see the line waves on the surface. As soon as I felt this, I gave the line back to Logan to continue with his fishing. The fight with the fish started; it was evidently something big. The fish would go under the canoe, and Logan would turn, and this happened repeatedly until he was utterly tangled up on the nylon line, from head to toe, and the fish continued to fight. We had to lay Logan on the canoe's floor, fasten him, cut part of the nylon around his body, and recover the fishing line. Then, the fish we had not seen jumped out of the lake, showing half its body. It was gigantic. It was the first paiche (*Arapaima gigas*) I had ever seen, and I was fascinated!!

While this turmoil was going on, the other two canoes approached. When we had recovered the line, and the paiche was close to our canoe, Elder Tukupi appeared on the small canoe with his son, who was trying to stab an artisanal harpoon into the fish, but it didn't go in. This scene repeated itself various times. The fight was vicious. Logan retook the line and fought the fish as we approached the riverbank because it was too big to lift into the canoe. Once at the riverbank, we beached the canoe on the swamp. We pulled the line and placed the fish in the mud. Logan, who was super excited and had bursts of adrenaline, jumped and sank in the mud on the third lower part of the fish. When he touched the fish, the paiche moved its tail and hit Logan, which forced him from where he was. We all jumped into the mud and pulled the fish out. Finally, Tukupi's son slammed a machete between the fish's eyes, and it slowly rested. We made a fire on the shore and took the fish, and while we rested, we prepared the fish. Its scales were so big that a knife couldn't enter them. An area must be descaled with a machete to introduce a knife to cut the meat. My surprise was enormous when I saw this giant's heart, which was as small as the heart of a rooster. There was no logical proportion between the fish's size and its heart. It was fascinating to see its organism, one of the biggest sweetwater fish in the world.

It produced around 80 pounds of meat. Elder Tukupi walked about 30 steps from the fire into the forest and, with the help of our lanterns, started to gather lianas and palm leaves. He built three large backpacks to transport the fish back to the community. When we arrived at Tukupi's house, the women started to cook part of the catch to make soup with yucca, Chinese potatoes, and green plantain. Most of the catch was smoked over wooden grills built over burning charcoal. We were exhausted, so while the women took care of the house chores and offered chicha, the fishermen rested.

We celebrated, rested, and shared with the community the next day. Many families arrived to bring some of the smoked paiche back to their homes. In the space of rest and celebration, we told Tukupi about the passengers' next part of the trip: hunting a bear in Alaska. When Tukupi heard the story and saw pictures of the grizzly, he told Logan and his father, Gowen, that it was the first time he had seen a bear. He was impressed by the size and its beauty and asked what the bear ate. The answer was many things: roots, plants, leaves, insects, forest fruits, animal carcasses, and newborn or very young moose. Bears are dangerous to humans. Tukupi was amazed to hear the bear stories while repeatedly looking at the marvelous animal's pictures.

The bear is an animal of power, like the anaconda. To kill such an animal is not good unless it attacks you, and you must defend yourself. Kill animals just for nourishment. If you kill a bear, you will lose your power, Tukupi told Logan. He got up, said farewell, took the pictures, and went to sleep. Logan was impressed by his words and looked at his father, expecting a comment, but Gowen said nothing. He got up and went to sleep. Surprised by his father's reaction, Logan looked at me, waiting for a comment. I got up, gave him a friendly pat, and told him to process what he had lived, to compare, especially how he felt at the moment concerning his previous expectations, and when he was ready to make a decision, to be honest with himself and to search for what was going to make him feel well with himself. On the farewell dinner in Quito, Logan asked his father to change their plan, to go to Alaska to observe the bears in their natural habitat and to be with them as much as possible, but not to hunt them.

Every time we visited Tukupi, his youngest son, Tarira, who was 8 years old, was one of the most outstanding characters. He was deaf and mute and had a deformity in his chest. His ribs formed a frontal protuberance, but he always smiled, playful and happy. He was always near his father. Also, you could see in the old man's seriousness and formality that his little son was the one who made him show his sensitive and loving side. One day, as I was in my office at Hotel Crespo in Cuenca, Tukupi's older son arrived suddenly, with Tarira very ill and almost unconscious. We took Tarira to the Emergency Department of Santa Ines without losing time. I called my doctor friends, who did everything possible to stabilize the child. Still, unfortunately, after a few hours of struggling, the little boy died. The speed and violence of how everything happened were devastating. In those days, the trip from Cuenca to Macas usually lasted 10 hours without counting unpredictable things like landslides, traffic accidents, heavy rains, mud, etc. The only way to reach Tukupi from Macas was by using the Missionary Air Service, which was the only transportation available and depended on the weather in the Amazon. That is why I suggested Tukupi's older son bury the child in Cuenca because it would take too long to reach Tukupi. He refused totally, saying that his father would punish him if he appeared without the body of the child. Nevertheless, after insisting and saying that I was responsible and telling my friend Tukupi that I was responsible for the child, he went home with sad news. We buried Tarira in a niche in the Municipal Cemetery of Cuenca, knowing that, according to the law, only after 5 years we could recover the body.

A few months after the burial, I visited Tukupi with a tourist group. He was stern and received me in a different way than in previous times. We sat in his tankamash (social area), he asked his wives to serve chicha, we drank, I greeted him and gave him my condolences for the death of Tarira, and he very seriously asked, "Daniel, what happened to my son?" I explained to him, in detail, what had happened and asked him to understand why I made that hard decision based on how difficult it would have been to carry the boy's body from Cuenca to Tukupi, and that in 5 years, I would bring Tarira's remains home so he could rest in peace. All this conversation occurred in front of the six passengers and the three wives of the elder, who cried gloomily with their brothers and sons. An excellent discussion started. Some said one thing, others said that if Daniel died, we would never see our little brother. It caused great polemics and controversy. At that moment, I was overwhelmed and felt the great responsibility I had taken. I felt a strong, genuine, and legitimate link with Tarira's family. It gave me something to remain with me for the rest of my life. It was a moment of "charging" something valuable and lasting. I made the trip from Miazal to Wichimi thrice a year, and we visited Tukupi for 2 nights each time. Each visit became part of the initial salute to ask me how his son was. I always answered that he was okay, not alone, and calm. And I would continue the visit with the tourists as usual.

Five years passed, and I had two consecutive groups with John Perkins. One included the Andes and Miazal, and then 3 days later, I started another excursion to Miazal- Wichimi, which offered an excellent opportunity to bring back Tarira's remains. I had to get the equipment ready and buy the food, so I asked my wife, Sarita, to do the paperwork on the Municipal Cemetery and recover the boy's remains. For Sarita, it was a rather unusual and somewhat strange task; nevertheless, she carried it out diligently and opportunely. She placed the rests in a little wooden box lined in blue velvet. I put the urn in a waterproof plastic container. When we approached the port to Tukupi's house, I was ecstatic knowing they would finally receive Tarira after a little more than a 5-year wait. I took the urn from the plastic container and placed it on my legs. I had advised my clients about the story from the beginning of the trip, so they were totally aware and equally excited to be part of this moment.

In the jungle, you can hear the noise of an outboard motor approaching from very far away. The children run to the shore to try to spot the boat coming. When the kids saw me with the blue urn on my legs, they knew immediately that I was bringing Tarira with me. When the canoe docked on the beach, Elder Tukupi and his three wives wailed with a sound that touched your soul; all the brothers and the extended family (clan) were already there. I asked the passengers to stay on the boat; I left the boat holding the urn in my hands and approached Elder Tukupi, extending my arms, and said, "Brother, time has gone by; here is Tarira." Tukupi placed his hands on the urn and asked me if Tarira's head was there. "Of course!" I responded. "Please open the box so you can see and make sure." "No," he said, "If you say so, it is okay." He received the urn, and tears came out of his eyes, but he kept his seriousness and temper. He asked me to let the tourists come down from the boat and build our camp outside his house, as we always did. There were lamentations from the women for hours. The community gathered in Tukupi's house to drink chicha and keep vigil over the child after a long time. It was a memorable visit.

When I returned with the next group a few months later, I was surprised to see the blue urn on a wooden board placed as a shelf on the roof. While we drank chicha, I asked Tukupi why it was there, and he answered that Tarira had been away from home for a long time. They wanted him to familiarize himself again with the smells and sounds of life in the house, listen to the voices of his mothers and brothers, and feel at home once again. He remained there for the next two trips (8 months). When it wasn't there anymore, I asked about the urn, and he said he had buried it under his bed.

My trips to Miazal with John Perkins for eight consecutive years were also memorable. We offered Shamanic Learning trips combined with visits to the Yachaks (shamans) of Imbabura in the Andes to do "limpias" (cleansings), then we would go to Miazal in the Amazon region to have Natem medicine ceremonies. Additionally, John offered psyconavigation sessions, using a drum played uninterruptedly while the participants relaxed and had a guided meditative journey.

The way I met John Perkins was interesting because he had lived in Ecuador before as a volunteer of the Peace Corps, working in the Morona Santiago province with indigenous and farming communities. One day, John was returning ill from the jungle and was walking on the road in Gualaceo, where we had an Inn. When my father saw him, he realized the young man was ill, so he offered to help him and took him to the doctor. My father offered him a place at the Inn to rest and get better. They became friends, and from then on, every time John left the jungle for Cuenca, he would visit my father, Don Henry. John finished his voluntary period and returned to the USA.

He returned in 1981 and wanted to visit my father. He went to Hotel Crespo in Cuenca, where we lived, and asked for Mr. Koupermann. He was taken to my office, announced, and came in. When he saw me, he was surprised and said he was sorry and was looking for Mr. Koupermann. I said I was him, and because of his surprise, I realized he was asking for my father. So, I told him that he was apparently looking for my father, who had died two years ago, and that I was in his place. That I was Daniel, his son. We started talking, and he told me how he met my father during his time in the Peace Corps. I told him I was in charge of the two family hotels and that, apart from that, I planned trips to the Amazon to the Shuar territory. He became interested because he worked with them as a volunteer and had lived experiences that marked him for life. But he also mentioned that he had worked organizing cooperatives for cattle development in the Amazon, to which I responded about the harm they had caused in the jungle and how it had been a mistaken proposal that had caused irreversible damage to nature, aggravating the problem of poverty in the families that now don't have forest nor cows and that the land was so poor in the Amazonia that after a few years of planting the soil became exhausted. John was surprised by my point and said that he didn't believe that had happened, so I invited him to the zone of Limon Indanza, Sucua, and the surrounding areas, where he had been some twenty years ago.

He traveled to the zone and saw only dried pastures, total deforestation, and no cows. He returned impressed and sorry, a little embarrassed upon seeing the negative impact of cattle farming in the Amazon. He asked me what he could do to try to repair what had happened in some way. I told him that I didn't know and that it was a good idea to go to Miazal and have a Natem (Ayahuasca) ceremony so that he could have his own vision and discover something. He liked the possibility and accepted the proposal. I organized a trip with Carlos Arcos, my associate and son of Doña Amalia, to take him to Miazal and have a ceremony with Tuntuam. He did it. He explored Miazal, visiting the giant waterfall and the trek to the thermal waterfall on the Tsuirim River. He returned to Cuenca happy and fascinated with the place and what he had experienced. He was relieved of his worry because of the ¨limpia¨ the medicine and the waterfalls had done to him. And through the vision he had, he concluded, as a way of compensating, he would bring groups of people (travelers, tourists) interested in the trips of Shamanic learning with the Indigenous cultures that I carried out, and that the money generated by the trips would be used in projects for the communities surrounding Miazal.

That is what happened; John brought groups for eight continuous years. When the first group arrived, he also took the medicine to thank them for having achieved his objective by following the vision he had had in his earlier visit. When John was under the effect of the medicine, he asked me to take him to the forest. I took him, and we entered. It was a moonlit night, and the light filtered through the canopy, creating light spots on the forest floor, almost like stars. John started touching the leaves of the plants around and crying, full of feelings, asking for forgiveness and telling the plants and the trees that he would take care of them.

For many years, the Natem ceremonies have been an essential portal for preparing and accompanying people during the ceremonies, watching over them, and attending them. I never take the medicine when caring for travelers to whom I facilitate the experience. I have also never, during all these years, given myself permission to prepare the medicine. I always offer this experience in the Amazonia with Uwishin (shamans), the ancestral custodians of the tradition.

This relationship I've had for years with the plant has allowed me to know the human condition from a particular perspective. It has allowed me to understand the immense power of the human mind, which creates so many ideas, illusions, fantasies, and fears that control and dominate lives. It has helped me understand that intelligence, the most precious and differentiating gift of our species, is, at the same time, the biggest obstacle to spiritual development, the biggest obstacle to living our sacredness and feeling as creatures that are part of creation and not the way humanity feels, separated from nature. Here is me and there, the world. When exposed to medicine, people become physically vulnerable; the majority surrender and try to acquire a vision. Others try to control the experience and do not surrender, losing the chance to receive the benefit. The medicine does not react the same with everyone; each person gets what they need.

In the same way, we visited the highland Shamans in the Andes Cordillera, especially in the province of Imbabura. The Tamayos, with Don Esteban and his son Jorge, are a true Yachak (shamans) lineage from Carahuela near Otavalo. Maria Juana, her husband Don Antonio, and their son Tarquino are in Aguarongo.

The cleansings "limpias"in the Andean tradition, are inspired by the presence of surrounding volcanoes and mountains known as Apus. The Yachaks carefully collect stones in the sense that the stones "call" the people. You feel that call, you ask for permission, and you collect the stones as if they were "huacas." During the limpias, the stones are passed through the patient's body to give the energy and power of the Apus. Before that, they use eggs, which pass through the body and the chakras. These eggs can absorb and remove illness and bad energy from the body.

Additionally, medicinal plants like nettle, datura, chilca, and others depend on the place. Blowing sugar cane liquor on the body and softly hitting the body with the plants facilitates blood circulation during the limpia, producing lightness. It is an ancient practice similar in all the Andean countries, with local variations.

The limpia intends to leave the body and mind in balance, harmonizing energies, taking out the bad, and incorporating the good. In the case of Imbabura, in Ecuador, candles are used at the beginning of the limpia. They are rubbed on the body, especially on the chakras. While this is being done, the person has to focus so that the candle absorbs the energy from the body. The candles are lit to diagnose, and the fire, with its shine, movement, size, and behavior, indicates the degree of interruption in the energy flow. At the end of the limpia, the candles are reread to see the improvement that should be reflected immediately. If, apart from the limpia, more treatment is needed to cure and heal specific problems, the patients are subjected to more extended stays, fasts, intake of specific medicinal plants, or specific limpias. On regular visits, there isn't enough time to follow those treatments, so some travelers return later to follow those healing treatments.

During the years I worked with John, he wrote some books: The World Is As You Dream It, Spirit of the Shuar, and Shape Shifting.

7. Achuar – Kapawi Ecolodge

I worked in Miazal until 1993, when I was invited to a board meeting at CANODROS SA, an Ecuadorian company in the city of Guayaquil, the most important port in the country. They operated luxury boat cruises with a capacity of 100 passengers to the Galapagos. They invited me because they wanted to discuss the development of an eco-touristic project in the Amazon.

They heard from an old friend, Guido Flavio Jalil, a board member, that I had experience doing adventure trips in the Jungle and was a hotelier. When Guido called to invite me, he gave me the profile of the Galapagos operation and the company's interest in extending its offer due to their vital market participation in the Islands. I went to the meeting at the Yacht Club on the boardwalk on the shores of the Great Guayas River.

I took advantage of the invitation and brought my project of a mountain lodge in the Cajas National Park, where I had started my condor-watching trips. This was the final project of two young architects, Marco Arias and Giovanny Cordero, who requested my assistance in developing the thesis. This project became one of my dreams at that time. We created a spectacular plan for a lodge in the middle of a *Polylepis spa* forest in Guagrahumag. This forest was like a fairy tale, with a small river running through the middle, disappearing under roots, rocks, and moss in certain areas. It was truly spectacular! It was also a structure with low environmental impact and, because of its operability, would contribute in an essential way to the park's conservation and facilitate regulated operations in the zone. I took the model and the master plan with the environmental impact studies to present at the board meeting. It was a business model with significant commercial and conservation potential because it was close to Guayaquil and Cuenca.

Don Carlos Perez Perasso was the CEO of CANODROS SA and El Universo, Ecuador's biggest and most important newspaper. My last name was familiar because he remembered my father, Henry Koupermann, and the Samarina case. The 5-star hotel on the Ecuadorian coast belonged to my father and was lost during the military dictatorship in the 70s. He had been a frequent client of the hotel's restaurant.

The first time he saw me, he told me he had known my father and remembered the great injustice done against him. That was the first moment in a long history to which I would dedicate 15 years of work, profoundly impacting my life and family.

The meeting started. Seven members of the Board read the agenda, and the only topic they would talk about was receiving my visit and discussing an idea they wanted to explore. They commented that they had been operating the M/N Galapagos Explorer, a tourist cruise ship with a capacity for 100 passengers, for many years in the Galapagos Islands. It was a successful operation with a significant international tour operator client portfolio. During the last year, they carried out surveys with the passengers. They determined that a substantial percentage of them combined the cruise around the Islands with a visit to the Amazon, which was evidently a preference of international visitors. Thus, they were interested in exploring the possibility of building and developing an ecotouristic operation in the Ecuadorian Amazon. They asked me what I thought about that possibility.

At that moment, I reflected that there were already some good quality Jungle Lodges, La Selva and Sacha Lodge, the leaders, along with some other excellent options in the Cuyabeno National Park. I took this moment to ask them to allow me to show them the Cajas project, which was more exciting and feasible. I made my presentation, and they showed attention and interest. Ultimately, Don Carlos told me he would tell me when he could visit the Guagrahumag forest. After a short time, Carlos called me and said that on the following Saturday, he would drive up to the forest from Guayaquil and meet me there.

He arrived with Commander Arnoldo Naranjo, Operations Manager of the M/N Galapagos Explorer. We walked around the forest filled with yellow orchids between the twisted branches. The atmosphere and natural beauty enchanted Don Carlos and the Commander, with whom we enjoyed a profound and gentle contemplation during the walk. At the end, he said: " Let's buy the forest immediately, but first let's do something in the Amazon, and then we'll build the Lodge in El Cajas. The land belonged to Don Oswaldo Quieroz and comprised 30 acres. A true gem!

I knew Don Oswaldo very well. He was the chief arriero (muleteer) and guide who worked with me on the Cajas tours. We used the Guagrahumag forest as a starting point for our expeditions. We acquired the land, but we could never carry out the project. The forest was inherited by Don Carlos Perez's three daughters.

Don Carlos told me that he was interested in my assistance in developing the Amazon project, but that before doing anything, he would like to visit the Jungle with me to make sure I knew about it and to confirm that I was the right person to contribute with the project, We prepared a trip to my organization in Miazal, to then travel through the Mangosiza, Morona, and Kaigaime rivers. My associate, Carlos Arcos, would wait for us with the aluminum boat in Miazal, where we would fly directly from Guayaquil on a Dornier Do 28 motor, the only plane authorized to fly that route.

The members of this expedition were Don Carlos, his son-in-law Mario Miraglia, the sales manager of Canodros, Rafael Lecaro, and his wife Maria Eugenia, Carlos Arcos, and I. It was only a 4-day trip because Don Carlos had little time. We arrived at Miazal early in the morning, loaded the boat with the equipment and supplies, and started our expedition downriver on the Mangosiza River. At 5 pm, we camped on an uninhabited shore. The Jungle's magic appeared, the sunset and the night sounds, the starry sky, and the stories of Shuar myths covered us and connected us with the greatness of the moment. We navigated the following day with short stops for fishing and having lunch on the shores. These were days for transmitting information about the ecology of the tropical rain forest and about the indigenous situation in their political and cultural aspects.

Don Carlos was thrilled. He had moments of profound reflection about himself, his life, and his position as one of the most powerful men in Ecuador at that time. He knew the country's problems, actors, and detractors profoundly. He used to say *Ecuador is a country made of paper and stuck together with saliva"*.

The following day, we continued navigating. We stopped at a lake to see alligators and take a short walk. We continued on the Cangaime River, and the afternoon reached us in the Kapaime community. We shored the boat, and Carlos went down to ask the Sindico, or leader of the community, for permission to camp on the shore. Shortly after, the Sindico appeared with Carlos, who wanted to welcome us and invite us to join them in the Assembly that was taking place at that moment, with the Association members formed by four communities. We thanked him for the invitation, unloaded the boat, set up camp, cleaned up, and approached the community house to assist, as auditing invitees, to the Assembly.

We introduced ourselves and were officially and formally received following the preestablished protocol. The Indigenous Amazonian organizations are based on the parliamentary system, where authorities are elected by popular vote and obey the dictates of the Assembly.

The formality of the procedures and the Assembly's dynamic, the seriousness with which some members participated, asking for the floor, and using it with total presence and responsibility. At the same time, the rest of the participants listened attentively without interrupting as the directors managed to grant the floor and make the official announcements, and how the decision-making and resolutions were counted through explicit votes simultaneously. In other words, democracy, manifested in its fundamental essence, impacted Don Carlos profoundly. Seeing the Shuar indigenous people, most of them illiterate, humbly living their lives in their communities, leading their Assembly with such dignity and propriety made a difference...When we returned to our camp, Don Carlos told me he would do anything with people like that...

The following day, we arrived at Puerto Napo, a new town created so the colonists from the southern Andes of Ecuador could find a better future because of the severe drought in the Andes, erosion, and minimal farming land. The government promoted colonization and cattle farming as an alternative for economic development and to overcome poverty. Our Dornier plane arrived, and we flew to Shell to refuel and then directly to Guayaquil. It was a lovely trip, and above all, it offered a perfect space to get to know Don Carlos Perez, who inspired confidence and security so that I could give the next 15 years of my life to construct the great project of my life, Kapawi Ecolodge in the Ecuadorian Amazon.

In the middle of 1993, I started exploring the Amazon for CANODROS. To the north of Imuya and Lagatococha, I visited Sacha Lodge and La Selva Jungle Lodge. I had no interest in the provinces of Sucumbios, Orellana, and Napo because of oil exploration and exploitation and their negative consequences on the environment and local communities. In the province of Morona Santiago, where I had worked for 12 years, there was an intense cattle farming development among the Shuar communities, so thousands of hectares were deforested yearly. New roads were opened for the latest development promoted by the government, such as San Jose de Morona, a pilot model community for people from the Andes. They were invited to colonize the Amazon and create a new town of colonists. They were assured land ownership based on the space each family managed to deforest to grow feed grass for the cattle and other intensive crops.

I overflew the province of Pastaza, which was unknown to me. We recognized the Bobonaza River, which, after Montalvo, was a primary forest with few Sacha Runas and Achuar communities. Suddenly, on the lower course of the Bobonaza, we saw a vast black lagoon next to the river. We flew in circles, recognizing the area, and it was a beautiful place that caught my eye. I asked Pepe Arcos, the pilot and an old friend of Miazal, to whom these lands belonged, and he confirmed that it was the Achuar and that the closest community was Chichirat.

*The Achuar formed part of the Shuar Federation, created in 1964. Since then, the Achuar were represented by the Shuar until 1991, when they decided to be recognized as a people and nation. The Achuar chose to form their own organization; months later, they formed the Oinae (Interprovincial Organization of the Achuar Nationality of Ecuador). The **OINAE was** legally recognized on November 5, 1993, by the Ministry of Social Welfare of that time. This change signified a significant advance towards opening new horizons and the participation of the Achuar people in politics.*

*In 1996, the OINAE changed its name to **FINAE** (Interprovincial Federation of the Achuar Nation in Ecuador). It maintained this name until April 2005, when it adopted the final name **NAE** (Achuar Nationality of Ecuador).*

In Puyo, I searched for the Directors of the Achuar. It was the first Board of Directors of the recently formed **OINAE** (Interprovincial Organization of the Achuar Nationality of Ecuador). The president was Luis Vargas; Ruben Tukup was the vice president; Alejandro Taish was the secretary; Domingo Peas was the treasurer. They represented the Achuar people, who occupied a territory of 1902711 acres. We met at Hotel Turingia. I introduced myself and told them that I had been making trips to Miazal and had frequently visited the Achuar community of Wichimi for many years.

Then I explained that I worked for CANODROS and was searching for a place to develop an ecotouristic project in the Ecuadorian Amazon. The company successfully operated a luxury cruise ship for 100 passengers in the Galapagos. It was an Ecuadorian company from Guayaquil, and the owner also owned the El Universo newspaper.

I commented that we had carried out an overflight of the Bobonaza River and the Lower Pastaza, and that a black lagoon in front of Chichirat and the mouth of the Capahuari River in the Lower Pastaza caught my eye.

For the Achuar leaders, my visit and a private company's interest in building an ecotouristic project on their territory were a real opportunity. A few months before, they achieved legal status and recognition for their organization. They talked amongst themselves in their native Achuar (Jibaro) for a long time, and they decided that their president (Luis Vargas) and vice president (Ruben Tukup) would accompany me on a trip to Chichirat. That afternoon, we contacted Negro Aragon by radio, an Afro-Ecuadorian married to an Indigenous woman who lived in Pacayaku for many years. Pacayaku was a Quechua community (Sacha Runa) on the Bobonaza River. He was the only person who had an outboard motor. We asked him if he would rent his canoe and motor to take us to Chichirat and perhaps Amuntai (Kapawi). He confirmed his availability and asked us to bring 30 gallons of fuel and oil for his Yamaha 25 HP outboard motor. The following day, we flew with the two leaders in a Cessna 172 and the fuel and supplies on another plane. We slept in Pacayaku in a schoolroom that was provided.

Very early the following day, we started our trip on the Bobonaza River until we arrived at the end of the day at the Achuar community of Chichirat. Since we were traveling with the leaders of the Achuar organization, we were very well received by the community and the Sindico (the highest authority of the Achuar communities, elected for 3-year periods). The communities were primarily incommunicado at that time. There were a few communities with HF radios to communicate with the outside world and within them. Thus, our visit was unannounced and a surprise for them. Luis Vargas talked to the Síndico about the purpose of our trip and requested to call a meeting. The majority of the community was present; we presented our interest in developing a project on the great black lagoon, which was close to the community on the other side of the river.

The Achuar's questions were: Why do you want to come here, where there is nothing? You must have some hidden intentions...The bad reputation of the white men weighed heavily, from the stories their grandfathers told about the rubber workers on the higher Bobonaza to those that cannibalized the Indigenous. These were stories that were repeated for many generations. At the end of the meeting and after a profound deliberation, they told us that they were not interested in the project and that we should follow our way the next day after having the guayusa tea.

Every day of their life, starting at 7 – 9 years old, the Achuar drink guayusa tea (*ilex guayusa*). Guayusa is a tree whose leaves are cooked. The lady of the house gets up between 3 and 3:30 am to warm up the fire for the tea cooked the night before. It is interesting to see how, at that time, the fires increased in each hut along the airstrip. At around 4:00 am, the family gathers around the teapot and starts drinking guayusa in an elongated bowl (pilche or Unkuship), which is exclusively used for the guayusa. The ritual begins with each person taking the Unkuship and serving some water, cleaning their mouths, gargling, and spitting behind on the earth floor of the hut. Then, each serves tea from the hot pot, partially submerging the Unkuship. You drink in silence with short, intermittent sips, in total silence. You drink and refill the bowl various times for an average of 20 minutes until your stomach feels full of liquid. You get up, walk outside for about 30 meters, and vomit with a leaf or with a finger. It is a daily stomach cleansing; make sure any leftover decomposed food is eliminated daily.

Additionally, due to its high caffeine and antioxidant content, it is a stimulant that provides energy quickly. It is absorbed through the stomach walls. Personally, it gives me a feeling of much energy and "lightness".

After vomiting, you return to the hut and once more use the Unkuship to serve a bit of water to wash your mouth, followed by spitting behind on the floor of the house. The men of the house, especially the adults, use this moment to groom their hair and paint their faces with achiote (*Bixa Orellana*) to look well-presented and ready for the day. The lady of the house serves warm cassava chicha, and the conversation begins while it is dark. The first light of dawn starts to light the day.

The custom of drinking guayusa is an ancient tradition of the Achuar people. It is a moment of family intimacy to share dreams each person considers important, make them known to the family, and receive advice and interpretation. Depending on the meaning given to the dreams, the person might avoid going fishing or hunting, or, on the contrary, do it. In the same manner, sometimes, the dreams might anticipate real-life situations. All families have a guayusa tree in their gardens or orchards.

It is also a moment to transmit the oral tradition to their children and teach them the necessary trades for daily life, such as fishing nets, harpoons, ceramics, weavings, crafts, etc. It is also a time to tell stories of trips carried out by family members, community events, memoirs and anecdotes, and repeating myths and legends generation after generation.

Decisions and problem resolutions in the family or community are made during Guayusa's time. Also, when guests are in the house, it is an honor to be invited to drink Guayusa with the host family.

Once, when I was in charge of the Achuar Air Service, I had a verbal dispute with an Achuar NAE leader. He was distraught with me because I had denounced the abusive use of the planes on his part, and he received a warning from the Board of Directors. He wouldn't answer my greetings or talk to me from that moment until the following year. His resentment was evident. The Annual General

Assembly of the NAE approached, in which I had to present my accountability to the plenary session of the Assembly, made up of approximately 340 representatives of all the communities of the Achuar territory.

Due to the importance that its AEROTSENTSAK Air Service represented for the Achuar Nation, it needed to be more politically correct for me as a Managing Consultant to maintain this disagreement. To apologize and ask for his contribution to the assembly agenda, I spoke to a friend from the community to ask him to allow me to serve a Guayusa at his house, paying for his wife to prepare tea for my guests. I invited six people, including the resentful leader, to a Guayusa to talk. We met and served the Guayusa according to tradition, where the owner of the house, not me, spoke about the intention of the meeting and marked the times of the ritual. I managed to get him to accept my apology, and we resumed an old friendship of 12 years since he took the naturalist guide course at Kapawi Lodge. What would life be like for the Achuar without Guayusa?

We continued our trip downstream along the Bobonaza River, a river with a million curves. The terrain is so flat that the water runs, forming a meandering channel with floodable banks and swamps. The Jungle at its finest, the walls of vegetation and trees, with shores never touched in thousands of years, of pristine and wild nature, can be seen as a chaos of branches, vines, leaves, and trunks, which are nevertheless in total balance, self-sustaining through millennia.

We arrived at the mouth of the Bobonaza River in the Pastaza River, which is gigantic, with a distance of 300 to 500 meters wide between banks, with deep areas and powerful eddies caused by submerged trees dragged in the floods. Sandbanks change position during the year and form sand islands along the channel. We arrived at the community of Kapawi on the left bank of the Pastaza. Known at that time also as Amuntai (The Achuar name for the bird Anhima cornuta, known in Spanish as Canclón and in English as Horned Screamer). In front of this community on the right bank of the river was the Captain Chiriboga military detachment.

The Kapawi community was made up of a group of Quichua and a group of Achuar families. The community's founders were 4 Achuar families and 2 Quichua families, one of them linked to the military as a canoeist and food supplier. This family maintained the political power of the community. Upon arriving with the leaders, looking for a place for the project with CANODROS, the community was very interested in the possibility of developing a project in their territory. We met with all the members the next day, and the project context was explained to them. Again, the same questions and doubts: what do you come to see if there is nothing here? They must have some hidden intention... They have to work for the oil company… With patience and effort, I responded to their concerns again. They agreed that they accepted the possibility and that I could stay a few additional days to explore the Capahuari River, where there were many lagoons. Because it was a smaller river, there were also more wild animals. We accepted the invitation, and we called by radio to request a flight for the leaders to go to Shell and bring in supplies for my exploration and fuel, and for the Negro Aragón to return to Pacayaku on the Bobonaza River from where we had departed.

The community designated Irar (Walter Vargas) as the person who would take me to explore the Capahuari River. Irar was the most prestigious hunter in the community and a great expert on every corner of the region. He was the son of a Shuar father and a Quichua mother; he had grown up with both cultures, spoke both languages , and was married to Doña Veneranda, a mestizo woman from the southern Andes of Ecuador in the province of Loja. Irar lived in two realities, one, the one that everyone in his family and community lived, and the other, his world of Ayahuasca, in which he explored his being and the spirits of the natural world of the Jungle. We spent the whole day with Irar waiting for supplies, enough time to get to know each other a little better and tell each other about what we have done in life and what we are looking for now; we talked about our families and our relationship with the spiritual world.

I shared ideas with him about what I was looking for to develop the Lodge project, such as access to lagoons, canals, streams in kayaks, trails through different types of forests, connecting small rivers with the great Pastaza River, and visiting families and communities. Imaginatively describing a day for the lodge passengers, from early morning bird watching and canoe rides at dawn on the river, walks, activities on trails, and visits to communities, until returning to the lodge, meetings with the guides about the activities and possibilities for the next day, socializing in bars and restaurants, and resting. I had to convey to him that what we wanted to offer our future passengers was a real experience and that we wanted to do everything with the least possible impact on the environment and the culture of the surrounding communities, which would be integrated into the project as a cultural component, adapting the visits and operation of the lodge to their cultural context.

Irar invited me to drink guayusa at his house the morning before departure. He told me about his hunting and fishing parties in the Capahuari River, the lagoons and swamps in its course, and the animals he had seen over the years. After the Guayusa, Doña Veneranda served Guanta (*Dasyprocta agouti*) broth with lots of meat, yucca, and plantain.

In those days, there was no outboard motor in Kapawi or the communities of lower Pastaza. In a medium-sized wooden canoe called a quilla (dugout canoe) made by hand from a Cedar trunk, with two seats, one in the stern and one in the bow, the load in the middle, we paddled the Capahuari River upstream. After 1 hour, the first mouth of a small river appeared, coming out of a lagoon near the shore. Walter told me that there are some lagoons like this in the River and that he thought the best thing was to paddle upstream for about 3 days and, from there, go down with the current, exploring the lagoons and swamps. At the end of the first day, we arrived at the mouth of the Kuzutkau River. On the second day, early morning, we navigated upstream and discovered spectacular mangroves and flooded jungle vegetation. We had to open a path many times for the canoe with our machetes since there were many fallen trees on the river. We discovered a virgin, untouched, pristine Jungle. In the middle of the afternoon, we arrived at the river, where it forms a lagoon, and we camped. The sounds of the night turned on, and the atmosphere became magical. Only the glow of burning firewood indicated the site of the camp; giant fireflies decorated the camp's surroundings with their light, and the profile of the trees was drawn in a starry sky, which dimly illuminated the deep darkness.

With the first light of dawn, the birds' colors and happy songs replaced the night's symphony of insects, bats, and frogs. At that moment, a continuity of sounds in that place had evidently been there uninterruptedly for millennia. We set up camp and continued exploring the Kuzutkau River upstream, where we found a family of giant otters (*Pteronura brasiliensis*) that were swimming curiously near the canoe, which was the signal to begin the return to the mouth of the Capahuari River and continue our exploration upstream to the house of Kayú, an Achuar warrior who lived with his two wives and some small children. He frequently visited the Kapawi community, where 4 of his children studied at school and three studied at the Wasakentsa mission on the other side of the Pastaza River. Over time, this place would become the community of Kuzutkau, which, as of 2020, has a population of approximately 120 people, all related to the sons and daughters of Kayú.

As we approached Kayú's house along the river, Irar took the shotgun and blew through the barrel, making a loud sound several times. When the house was visible, he did it again, ending with a cry, ¨Wiñaaaaaaaje¨ (Here I arrive); after a while, children came out to the shore to look curiously at who had arrived. In the Achuar culture, it is crucial to announce yourself from afar before approaching a house; failure to do so is bad manners and will raise suspicion and discomfort in the homeowner. Upon reaching the shore, Kayú appeared at the top of the shore, recognized Iriar, and greeted us with a ¨Vinitia yatsuru ¨ (Come, brother). Our arrival was not announced; Irar exchanged a few words with Kayú, who invited us to his house. Kayú took a seat in the place corresponding to the house's owner. He sits in a place that marks an imaginary line, approximately one-third of the way at the end of the oval of the house. The space behind the owner is exclusively for the family, where the family beds and the central kitchen fire are, where the chicha is kept.

The "Nijimianch" cassava chicha is the basis of man's survival in the Jungle. It is a drink obtained by cooking the root of the cassava (***Manihot esculenta)*** and then making a puree with some wooden paddles while it is still hot. They chew and mix the puree with their saliva and spit it back into the container, which they continue beating while repeating the process for about two hours, which is how long it takes each family to make chicha every day. In the Amazon, the water has sediments and microorganisms, so people only drink chicha. It has a high carbohydrate content and provides energy immediately, quenches thirst, and suppresses hunger. If it rests for two or more days, it ferments and becomes an alcoholic drink for specific celebrations.

In front of Kayú's seat (tutank), one-third of the house is the social area or Tankamash, where visitors are received. The Achuar house has no walls and a large oval roof up to 1.60 from the ground. Kayú asked his wives to offer us chicha, the traditional drink. There was silence and waiting while one of the ladies first served her husband and then provided a pinink or ceramic container to each of us; at that moment, the house's owner invited us to drink, after which the conversation ensued. Following protocol, Irar told Kayú who I was and why I was with him, then he detailed what we found since we left Amuntai by canoe, the exploration in the Kuzutkau River, which is part of his territory. Then, Irar described the idea of the ideal site and the activities that would be undertaken by the visitors. Kayú considered the information received and told us to unload the canoe to spend the night in his tankamash, where he asked us to assemble our mosquito nets and prepare a place to rest. We prepared dinner of rice with sardines and spent the night with a soothing rest. That afternoon, a little before dinner, Irar asked Kayú for space at one of the house fires to cook the Natem vine (Ayahuasca) and the Yaji (Chacruna) leaves he had brought on the trip. He sang an Icarus, placed the crushed vine at the bottom of the pot, and placed the Yaji leaves on the Natem. He blew wild tobacco smoke while he whistled his Icarus and spoke to the plants, asking for their presence and support for the purpose of the trip. He added water and cooked over low heat for about 6 hours without adding more water, resulting in a reduction. He regularly approached the pot, whistled, and blew tobacco; he was always present in the cooking, invoking his power animal, a black jaguar that is always present in his visions when he uses Natem/Ayahuasca. Irar receives his power from the black jaguar; his presence confirms his well-being, knowing he is protected.

At dawn, we shared guayusa; Kayú recommended we go upstream to certain places. We continued for one more day, drinking only water all day, fasting for the evening ceremony, and camping at the mouth of a lagoon. During the tour of the Capahuari River those days, we had observed a large amount of fauna, black caiman (*Melanosuchus niger*), capybaras (*Hydrochoerus hydrochaeris*), pink dolphins (*Inia geofrensis),* large groups of capuchin monkeys (*Cebus albifrons*), howler monkeys (***Alouatta palliata aequatorialis***), squirrel monkey (*Saimiri sciureus*), and on the *beaches and walks we found traces of jaguar (Panthera onca) and tapir (Tapirus terrestris*). A great variety of birds and fish. Likewise, the trees of an infinite variety from the giant and predominant Ceibos (*Ceiba petandra),* Fig trees (*Strangler fig*), Balsam trees (*Myroxylon balsamum*), Balsas (*Ochroma pyramidale*), Guarumos (*Cecropia*), and the Guabas (*Inga edulis*) with their white flowers hanging over the river, and hundreds of species of trees and plants that I didn't recognize. The abundance of everything always overwhelmed me; I felt in Eden, in an unknown land, untouched or undisturbed, still, calm, mine.

Irar served Natem (Ayahuasca) that night because we would go downstream the following day to explore each mouth and lagoon. It was essential to ask permission, receive vision, and tune in to Arutam, the spirit of the Jungle. For the ceremony in the camp, we did not make a fire, only candlelight, until we took the medicine. Then, it was total darkness, illuminated only by the stars and the moon.

My intention and purpose were to be grateful for being where I was, being "touched" by the energy of the Jungle, and finding the right place for the project. I felt that it was mandatory to submit to the will of the Universe, to the medicine, to the spirit of the Jungle, to let it happen, without my will or preference being present that night... submit and trust, that was the feeling that took me to the ceremony. Thank you and ask for permission, thank you and ask for permission, thank you and ask for permission was the initial resonance in me, like a mantra, focusing on thanking and asking for permission... In my vision, the giant waterfall appeared from the ceremony with Doña Amalia and the Elder Chumpi in Miazal…that waterfall and that moment presented themselves vividly. I felt glad for the familiarity and clarity of the waterfall again. I entered the pool that formed under the waterfall, swam through it, and reached the waterfall; I entered the waterfall and let the water fall on me; the sound of the water and the sensation of the water drops on my head, shoulders, and back lasted forever. I became one with the waterfall, and when I looked behind the curtain of water in the cave, there was a large black Jaguar… Irar? The jaguar looked at me seriously, and he got up and left very slowly;

I followed him, and we walked through the Jungle on a starry night... I just followed him, without words, in total silence; from time to time, he turned to look at me and continued on his way, like guiding me through this, his world.

Early in the morning, Irar asked me if I was happy and if I had asked for permission. I replied that I did and that a black Jaguar accompanied me in my vision. Irar smiled discreetly and told me: I know... During all these days in the Capahuari River, we saw pink dolphins almost every day in small groups of up to 6 individuals, which showed the excellent state of the environment. That morning, when we boarded, a group of them was swimming very close to the shore; we stayed motionless watching them, and the dolphins also stayed watching us; it was a genuine contact of mutual recognition.

Sailing downstream, we visited the first lagoon, entering with the keel through the mouth as far as the vegetation allowed us. A second and a third lagoon, entering all the lagoons, and exploring them. Some lagoons have large bodies of water and channels of vegetation, as well as islands of palms with thorns. Most of them had dry land shores with small hills. All beautiful, all magical. We camped on the bank of the river or in the mouth, where it caught us at 5 pm. On the 6th day, we arrived again at the mouth of the Kuzutkau River; we explored the terrain on foot at the mouth and in two places further inland. I had a strong feeling about that place and thought that this could be the ideal. On the 7th day, we left Kuzutkau and descended Capahuari again; we passed by Kayú's house, and one of his wives told us that he had gone to Amuntai to discuss our visit and exploration and to wait for our arrival. We were exhausted when we visited about two more lagoons and continued paddling downstream. It was our 8th day of paddling, with a few provisions and drinking only filtered water. Irar came in the stern of the canoe, and I was in the bow in total silence. We paddled in silence, and suddenly, a dolphin appeared next to the canoe; we expected to see a group, but the dolphin was alone; it was probably a young adult male. He accompanied us by submerging and appearing on both sides of the canoe; with Irar, we only looked at each other, smiling at the company. Suddenly, the dolphin entered the mouth of the Guayancancocha lagoon. Irar, without saying anything, followed the dolphin and entered its mouth. I thought Irar was looking for a place to spend the night since it was late afternoon. A beautiful canal connects the Capahuari River with this lagoon. In those days, the lagoon had a large mirror of water, moderately deep and non-floodable shores; the afternoon was falling, so we approached the eastern shore that Walter knew (it was part of his hunting and fishing reserve); it was full of vegetation. We cleaned with machetes and went up to the shore about 4 meters (13 feet) above the water; we found a flat area and set up the tent facing West. We saw the lagoon and observed the dolphins feasting on abundant fish. A sunset with intense colors, the profile of the giant trees on the opposite shore, a mirage of three-dimensional clouds in pastel colors, was a moment... Night came, and the moon fell before us, forming a light beam on the water. The dolphin continued swimming through the beam of light in one direction and another.

Walter said that the dolphin had already eaten enough and that it was strange that it continued swimming in front of us. He felt that the dolphin was trying to tell us something. A messenger presented itself that way, and we should pay attention. I was surprised that what Irar said could be a possibility. We took Natem to confirm if the dolphin was communicating something or if it was a signal that we should understand. According to Achuar tradition, dolphins and hummingbirds are messengers of the Shamans.

The night was unforgettable. The dolphin stayed in my vision all night. Many Indigenous faces appeared older, people, adults, and children. The Guayancàncocha lagoon welcomed me. I felt accepted. It was the place indicated by the dolphin and the spirit of the Jungle. Irar agreed. It seemed logical to him since the lagoon was near the mouth of the Capahuari River in the Pastaza River. It made sense; it was organic to build the lodge there.

We explored the lagoon all day, and Irar located me on the ground. We walked about 250 meters to the Capahuari River, showing me where we should build the main dock and how the river was connected by land to the lagoon. Then we walked around the lagoon, finding two swamps connected to the lagoon, which were natural rainwater drainage systems that fed the lagoon. Following the shore towards the Northwest, we found a salt pond for tapir and peccary (White collar peccary), then a swamp with mangroves that connected this lagoon with a smaller neighboring lagoon, which in turn connected with another lagoon known as Lobococha, by the presence of otters in it. We continued walking along the shore and reached the other side of the access channel through which we entered with the dolphin and the canoe. We found a giant Ceibo tree, which to this day arouses admiration in those who visit it. Second night in Guayacancocha after having explored it from inch to inch and understanding its configuration. I fell into a deep sleep; we were exhausted.

The next day, we continued downstream to the mouth and from there to the community, where they were waiting for us to report the result of our exploration. The Leaders received us, offered us chicha and something to eat, and scheduled us to meet with everyone at 5 pm.

Irar took the floor and spoke in the Achuar language, detailing the trip and the ideal site for the project; according to the long conversations we had had about it during the journey, he detailed the exploration at length, including the presence of the dolphin. In the end, there were many comments and questions of all kinds, which I answered and were translated by the Sindico. There was a group of the most significant founders of the community, Wampush, Pando, Hilario, Gualinga, Manya, Calisto, and Kayú, who, upon hearing about the dolphin, felt comfortable, calm, and sure that the topic of the project was positive for the community. When they spoke, the community unanimously agreed. They asked me to communicate their resolution to the FINAE leaders in Puyo, and that they hoped the leaders would continue with the project.

The flight to leave for Shell arrived early in the morning. At the same time, I flew and contemplated the grandeur of the Amazon jungle and the giant clouds around the plane. I felt moved, excited, and happy about everything I had experienced in the last two weeks. I arrived at the Hotel Turingia in Puyo and called President Luis Vargas. I asked him to come to the Hotel Turingia with all the available leaders to meet in the afternoon. I had time to enjoy a steak with two fried eggs and nap for about 3 hours until the leaders arrived.

I summarized everything that happened since Luis Vargas and Rubén Tukup left me in Amuntai two weeks ago, especially my pleasure at the place we found and the attitude of the Amuntai community to whom the territory belonged. We had found the ideal place for the project. From there, two priority topics were raised to resolve the conversation:

How can a proposal be submitted to CANODROS SA so that they can invest in an indigenous territory where land sale is not allowed?

How do we present the project to the Achuar people? For the leaders, it was the first significant project of their newborn organization, OINAE.

We analyzed different alternatives and scenarios all afternoon until late at night. Regarding the approach to the corporation, the following proposal was reached: that CANODROS make the investment without purchasing the land and that it manage and control the operation for 15 years, enough time for them to recover the investment and time necessary for the Achuar to learn to manage the hotel and tourism business; after which the corporation would transfer ownership and operation to the Achuar nation. From the beginning of the public operation, CANODROS would also pay a monthly rent of $1,200 per month, with annual increases according to the inflation of the country's economy.

The approach to the Achuar people was based on the context of the nation at that time. When they began their organizational and political life, only four Associations and 14 communities made up the OINAE. Some communities and Associations continued to belong to the Shuar Federation. (They joined the OINAE gradually, seeing that the organization's management differed from other indigenous organizations.) Today, there are 16 Associations and 84 communities.

According to the political tradition in indigenous organizations, the leaders cannot make certain decisions without the consent of the General Assembly. The authorization for the leaders to finalize the agreement with the corporation had to be granted by the bases, represented in the said Assembly, which takes place once a year and in which members of all the communities of the Achuar Nation participate. Therefore, the strategy for the project was to visit the communities and socialize the idea of the "alternative economic development project" for the Achuar Nationality of Ecuador. The project belonged to all the Achuar, and all the associations and their communities were its owners. Once communities agreed, were informed, and consulted, leaders could gain approval from the General Assembly.

The leaders asked for the next day to talk among themselves and consult with the organization's advisors. They revisited me at the hotel at the end of the afternoon to confirm the general proposal and provide details of how they planned to distribute the rent they would receive. The important thing is to present the project as that of all the Achuar so that the job offer and a part of the monthly income would reach the 4 Associations. Equally important was the possibility of learning and educating in tourism management and, through this, becoming self-sufficient in the territory's economic development.

I felt comfortable with the group work's result in formulating the proposal's basis. I returned home to Cuenca to rest and digest everything that had happened. It was happening in a way in which my will was only a part of it, which added to other wills and produced the advancement and definition of the project. During those days at home, my vision was consolidated. I could clarify what I was looking for personally by seeing myself involved in this project.

1. It was an opportunity to fulfill my deep desire to give back to the indigenous people of the Amazon for what they taught me in the years I spent in Miazal with the Shuar and Achuar.

2. Likewise, "really" turning Ecotourism into a tool for the conservation of the Amazon forest, with which I had cultivated a relationship of admiration and inspiration, which brought me in such a unique way to the Natural History of our big house, The Earth.

3. To build a place to receive visitors and offer them a truly authentic experience in one of the world's most pristine and beautiful places.

4. To grow professionally, work for a large corporation, and offer a better future to my children. At that time, Jonathan was 11, Joel was 8, and Ilán was 1 year old.

It was also interesting because it was a completely new alternative proposal. At that time, there was no other project anywhere else to serve as a model. Indigenous organizations were politically identified with leftist movements. Three years before, there was an indigenous uprising in Ecuador (May 28 and June 4, 5, 6, 1990) under the title, "Mandate for the defense of life and rights of ¨indigenous nationalities." They occupied the church of Santo Domingo in Quito. Thousands descended from the mountains in the Andes. Thousands ascended from the Amazon and closed all the roads, leaving the cities completely unsupplied. Until then, the indigenous people were invisible in Ecuadorian society, which suddenly discovered that its food sustenance came from this class of Ecuadorians who had existed marginally without being part of the democratic process and practice. The uprising occurred months after the fall of the Berlin Wall.

Some of the postulates of the uprising were Rejecting the policies of the IMF, demanding the officialization of the languages of the indigenous nationalities of Ecuador through a constitutional reform, supporting the campaign for the 500 years of resistance against the colonialist celebration of the "Meeting of two worlds." demanding the suspension of territorial displacements in the Amazon, and requesting the definitive expulsion of evangelical institutions, such as the Summer Institute of Linguistics.

*The **recognition of the Plurinational State**, access to water sources, and land legalization, among other points. The government of social democrat Rodrigo Borja set up dialogue tables with the leaders, among whom were Luis **Macas, Blanca Chancoso, Valerio Grefa, and Nina Pacari**. It is worth emphasizing that Indigenous territorial rights were dramatic despite the agrarian reforms that had previously been carried out in 1964 and 1973. Impoverishment and displacement continued to be a constant in the communities, a situation that became unsustainable in the nineties. By Adriana Rodríguez Caguana, "Ecuador, 25 years of the first indigenous uprising" – June 4, 2015.*

So, alliances or joint ventures of indigenous organizations with private companies, in a business model without paternalism, needed a context for them to happen.

I went to Guayaquil to inform the CANODROS board, which was made up of seven people: Don Carlos Pérez Perasso and six people he trusted, businessmen in various areas, with whom he had managed the operation of the luxury cruise in the Galapagos Islands.

I informed them about the exploration that began three months ago when I went with Rafael Lecaro, Sales Manager at that time in

CANODROS, who accompanied me to explore the Lagartococha River on the northern border, in the areas of the Imuya River, about the exploration in the Aguarico River, about the visit to the lodges that were already operating very successfully on the Napo River and that would be direct competition for our project, finally about the exploration of the Bobonaza River and the lower Pastaza River with the Achuar (there were no cell phones at that time so they saw a few photos printed on paper).

When I had to communicate the reasons why the site was chosen, the main arguments were:

1. The place's isolation can only be reached by flying in small planes; the pristine nature of the place, without the presence of livestock or colonization.

2. The diversity of the plant and topographic formations of the area: large and small rivers, white and black water lagoons, permanently flooded forest (igapos), dry land forest, varzea forest (flooded in one season of the year), swamps, that is, a true mosaic of Amazonian formations and ecosystems in an area of a maximum of 4 hours from the place, in any direction. Most Amazonian ecosystems occupy vast areas, so having this variety so close to each other was a plus for the site.

3. The Achuar communities in the project's area of influence will allow us to authenticate the cultural component without any folklorism. These communities have not had contact with non-Achuar people except for missionaries and occasionally soldiers who patrol the border area with Peru.

4. The excellent reception by the Amuntai community, which was closest to the project and owners of the territory where we would build and operate.

5. The proximity to large rivers, navigable by motor canoes (Pastaza and Bobonaza).

6. Convert the ecotourism project into a powerful tool for conserving the Amazon Forest and the culture of its inhabitants.

The most apparent difficulty and risk was using small planes to enter and leave. Still, it was also one of the differentiating elements from the other lodges in the Ecuadorian Amazon.

When they heard the association proposal, the board members became active in giving their opinions since the point caused a lot of friction. It was an unorthodox proposal that sounded like mental alienation.

The company could invest according to its criteria without purchasing the land and operate the business for 15 years, after which the operation and ownership would be transferred to the Achuar Nationality of Ecuador, represented by its organization OINAE. Additionally, the company will pay a monthly rental fee that will increase annually according to inflation.

These 15 years will be a magnificent opportunity for the Achuar to learn to operate, manage tourism, and maintain the operation in the long term, creating sources of work for the communities. The business proposal aimed to help the Achuar learn how to run a business. It was not the paternalistic model of the good guys helping the "poor indigenous people."

This concept was necessary for the context that CANODROS operated one of the most luxurious ships in the Galapagos, with a capacity for 100 passengers, so conceiving and implementing the project in the Amazon under this equation would contribute enormously to the company's image in terms of social and environmental responsibility and would offer the international market two exclusive destinations with high-quality services, differentiating themselves from the other companies with which they competed.

The idea of making a significant investment in a strange land and handing over the business after 15 years was not digestible for most directors; it was a concept that did not fit into their business. Each of them spoke to reinforce that the thesis was not viable.

Don Carlos Pérez, president of the board of directors with the majority of the share package, listened carefully to each of the directors; when everyone spoke, he took the floor and, arguing about the values of the proposal, said, "We are going to do it," it is worth it...

The directors looked at each other, and knowing Don Carlos, they knew there was nothing more to say. This was one of the moments in my life when, again, the presence of another will was added to mine to make things happen. I will always remember that event.

We organized a new trip so that Don Carlos could get to know the chosen place. This time, only Commander Arnoldo Naranjo, Operations Manager of Canodros, accompanied him. We flew again on the Dornier from Guayaquil directly to Shell; we changed to a smaller Cessna 206 plane and flew to Amuntai; we stayed at the guest house on the hill where the Mission is today. We saw the entire community below the hill, surrounded by a jungle with colorful sunsets. We visited the Guayancancocha lagoon by rowing canoe; we entered through the mouth, where we remembered the story of the dolphin who guided us there. We went to the shore where we had made camp with Irar; we walked along the nearby beaches and the path that connects the lagoon with the Capahuari River, to where we would make the main port of the project. I visualized and communicated ideas on occupying the place and making the lodge with cabins of vernacular Achuar architecture adapted to provide the greatest possible comfort. A viable, sustainable development model exists from using solar energy and 4-stroke outboard motors to conceiving a hotel and tourism operation with low environmental and cultural impact.

The imaginary description of the operation touched a personal chord with Don Carlos. He was really pleased with the idea and the possibility of doing it. He saw the project as a perfect complement to the operation in Galapagos. However, he also shared his feeling that he had received (or taken) so much from life that he felt he had to reciprocate and give something back somehow. The conception of

Kapawi Ecolodge created a space for Don Carlos to express his feelings and commitment.

The next thing was to move forward with the project. We hired architect Cornelio Montesinos to help us with the design. I took him to Kapawi to learn about the site and do the respective topographical surveys. It was important for the architect to know the concept of traditional vernacular housing of the Achuar in order to develop comfortable hotel rooms with private bathrooms and balconies overlooking the lagoon, based on the Achuar house, with the exact use of the same materials. This was very important in the concept of cultural impact that the infrastructure development be what the Achuar identify as their own and that they are the project's builders.

I coordinated with the OINAE leaders to continue with the socialization process. It was also essential to follow the protocol that the Achuar have in managing their organization: consult with the bases by presenting the project to the different communities and then submitting it to the popular will in a General Assembly. We planned a series of trips to other communities, most of which were headquarters of the Associations, which at that time were only four in the entire Achuar territory.

Luis Vargas, Domingo Peas, Rubén Tukup, and I were always on the presentation team. I prepared a slide presentation to project on a portable screen powered by a 2 KW gasoline generator. The photos showed the skyscrapers of New York, Hong Kong, Chicago, the Metro, and train stations to show how people who want to visit the Amazon live. People who get up early, have breakfast on the run, take an elevator down to the street, go down a tunnel, and go underground to take a train, which takes them to a station near another building with another elevator, to go to the office to work 8 to 10 hours, and return home the same way...every day... These people want to escape to nature and get to know cultures still in contact with the natural world. On one occasion, someone asked where the bathrooms were; it seemed incomprehensible when I explained that there were small rooms in the bedrooms or the living room next to the apartment's dining room. It was a source of laughter, knowing there were no chickens and everything they ate had to be bought with money.

Likewise, photos of the residential neighborhoods of cities in the USA and Europe, where there are mainly families who also want to travel the world, getting to know places and cultures at least once a year.

Also, we discussed the type of tourism we do not want, photos of the beaches of Ipanema and São Paulo with thousands of bathers, and pictures of the lines at Disneyworld to show mass tourism. We also showed images of tourism in the national parks in Costa Rica and African safaris to observe animals as an example of more selective tourism linked to nature. Photos of tourism in the Amazon with examples of the Flotel Orellana, Sacha Lodge, and Lodges in Peru and Brazil.

In addition to the photos and pertinent explanations, the main ideas that were transmitted in the presentations were:

1. The project would be an excellent opportunity for allies to develop other community projects.

2. Provide work for members of all Achuar communities during the construction and operation of the Lodge.

3. Learn to operate and manage the tourism business as an alternative for long-term economic development.

4. Stimulate and recover traditional crafts and generate a source of economic income for women and families in the communities.

5. Since the lodge opened to the public, the organization and the four associations have received a monthly income from the rental fee.

6. Demonstrate to the Ecuadorian State the positioning of the Achuar territory with important projects as evidence of protecting it from extractive oil, logging, and mining exploitation.

We visited the communities of Pumbuentsa, Wampuik, Charapacocha, and Amuntai, where representatives of Wayusentsa, Sharamentsa, and Ishpink arrived. The Association headquarters had HF radios with daily contacts, so the visit was communicated through that medium, inviting most people to participate. Covering all these communities took us about 6 months. It was an excellent opportunity to get to know the Achuar so that they could better understand the idea of the proposal, and for the Achuar to know me as the person in charge and executor of the project. These presentations were critical so that the Achuar had a rough idea of what it would be like and what it entailed to implement the project in their territory. Understanding and accepting tourism as a viable alternative to bring an economy to the territory and conserve its land and culture opens a new possibility in the minds of the majority. These were the communities from which the workers for the lodge construction would come, which was necessary for the appropriation that the Achuar would make over time of Kapawi Ecolodge as "their project."

Once presentations were made to all the associations, the Achuar had their Annual General Assembly, at which a presentation was again made, and approval to move forward with the Kapawi Ecolodge project was put to a vote. The leaders were authorized to proceed with formalizing the relationship and details of the alliance with CANODROS SA.

The architectural design was completed, precisely reproducing the structures of the Achuar house, with adaptations for a private bathroom, open closet with shelves, sleeping area with mesh windows without glass to connect with the sounds of the jungle, and a balcony over the lake with hammock and deck chair oriented towards the sunset, achieving an incredibly cozy space attached to the forest and the elements. The cabins were on the flooded shore on stilts, following the contour of the lagoon so that there was water under the floor when the river rose; you could swim around the structures.

We formed an essential work team with Cuny, the architect, the master carpenter Rafael García, four carpenters from Cuenca whom he trusted, and María Reyes as logistics coordinator at Shell. We initially hired approximately 90 Achuars from various communities to clean the lake shore and the 250-meter (800-foot) path, which connected to the main dock on the Capahuari River and the path from the pier to the staff quarters and outboard motor garage, another 150 meters (450 feet).

We rented several large houses in the community of Amuntai, where the workers lived. We also installed a carpentry shop on the bank of the Pastaza River, next to the community, with a small barracks for the teacher, Rafael, and his team, and occasionally the architect and a small office room for me.

Once the replanting of the cabins and the main paths was done, the task was to obtain the wood for the construction; the areas were identified where it was known that there was Balsam wood (**Myroxylon balsamum**), which is almost incorruptible due to oil and high molecular density. Likewise, we had to collect a large number of Pambil palm trees (**Iriartea deltoidea)**, an essential and multipurpose material used for the rods that give the elliptical shape to the roof, to make the walls, and to make staves that, once polished, gorgeous black floors with light veins were obtained.

The other basic materials were a variety of aerial roots used to tie the wooden pieces of the roof and the poles where the palm leaves were woven. The leaves for the roofs were one of the most sensitive materials. The best leaf is the palm, locally called Turuji, which grows in limited quantities in each place where it is found. You must make long journeys to see these places with very little Turuji palm.

The problem on the construction site was that there needed to be canoes large enough or sufficient to collect wood and transport the workers and the supplies we had to move between the airstrips to the construction site. The existing canoes were simply canoes for family use. It became a priority to solve this problem. I went to Coca in the northeast, where there were large wooden boats; I toured the docks and found about six canoes in good condition. On average, they were 16 meters long by 1.30 meters wide, and others were 12 meters long by 1 meter wide. I bought the canoes and rented platforms with mule trucks; we moved the canoes by road to Puyo and from there to the point where a planned route to Canelos ended at the head of the Bobonaza River. We unloaded the canoes in the pasture at the end of the dirt road. From there, we pushed by hand on logs for a day to Canelos, where the Bobonaza River was half a meter deep and, little by little, a little deeper until it became navigable. By oar and lever, after two days, we arrived at Pacayaku. In this Quichua community, I rented the canoe with a 25HP motor from Negro Aragón at the beginning of the exploration. We received the 40 HP outboard motors that arrived in small planes and would be used in large canoes. We continued along the Bobonaza River through the Quichua communities of Sarayaku, Montalvo, Boberas, and the Achuar community of Chichirat until the mouth of the Pastaza River. From there, we crossed it upstream to the Capahuari River, where the work was located.

Initially, we needed Balsam wood for the pilings and floor beams. Fortunately, just when we started construction, there was a group of dissident families from the Ishpingo community who were beginning to build a new community they called Wachirpas, located on the shore, right off the Pastaza River, 40 minutes downstream from the mouth of the Capahuari River. As we had some workers from this group of families, we were able to reach an agreement whereby we helped them cut trees and clear space for the community, communal areas, and landing strips for small planes, which are vital for all the communities in the interior of the Ecuadorian Amazon. In exchange, they gave us the Balsam and Pambil wood in the clearing. This alliance with the Wachirpas community gave us 80% of the wood for the job.

Collecting materials from the surrounding forest became the main activity for some time. The moment in the early morning was special; when the workers drank guayusa before the shift, they shared if they had any bad omen dreams. They painted their faces with seeds from the annatto plant (*Bixa Orellana*) to protect them during the shift. In the mornings, this ritual was daily; we organized groups of 6 to 8 men in different canoes, and we left in different directions.

At the end of the day, the groups returned to the carpentry shop, where the wood was selected and stored in an orderly manner for drying and processing the pieces already cut for the construction site. All the cuts and preparation of the wood were done in the carpentry shop and installed in the Amuntai (Kapawi) community to avoid making a lot of noise in the lagoon and have as little impact as possible. Likewise, the workers remained in the lagoon until 5 in the afternoon. Then everyone went to Amuntai, where the main camp was.

We had two kitchens, one in the Amuntai community, in a small house where it was also the food warehouse, and another in the lagoon that was only for lunches. Breakfasts and dinners in the community and lunches at work. The Achuar diet comprises carbohydrates, mainly cassava, tarot (Chinese potato), banana, and other tubers such as yams and pelma. There was good fishing that we bought from the natives of the nearby communities, especially Catfish of different types; the most appreciated was the Giant Catfish or Súngaro (*Brachyplatystoma rousseauxii)* that could weigh up to 100 kilos, and the Surubi Catfish brindle (Pseudoplatystoma reticulatum), which were equally of good size. For breakfast, usually fish soup with cassava, potato, or cooked banana. Rice with animal protein such as sardines, tuna, and mortadella was served for lunch and dinner. It was important to properly feed the workers, which Luchito Peñafiel, the cook, was responsible for with his Quichua assistant Julián Illanes. Luchito was a cook in mountain and jungle camps for several tourism agencies. Julián, who learned to cook, eventually became a chef, worked as a kitchen assistant at Kapawi Lodge for three years, and then, with practice, was transferred to the Galapagos Explorer cruise ship II, where he became a professional chef. We served large portions to compensate for the tremendous physical effort that the workers made. Likewise, for the Achuar, eating rice was a privilege and a delight since they did not consume it regularly. The elders of the new community of Wachirpas, under construction, when they talked with the workers of their community, who told them about the significant portions of food we served, said they were convinced that we were fattening them to make canned fish like tuna. These stories were remnants of tales transmitted orally from the time of the rubber tappers, who enslaved and mistreated the indigenous people so much. The workers returned to the work site to discuss these stories of the elderly with others, which forced me to visit them in Wachirpas to clarify and deny these stories, which caused concern among the workers.

Hilario Saant was the only Achuar with about five cows; he had learned from the Achuar of Morona Santiago and promoted livestock farming in the territory. During all the previous years in the Amazon, I learned and verified that livestock farming was one of the greatest environmental problems and a cause of destruction of the tropical forest. Hence, the Kapawi conservation project was an imminent risk. I tried fiercely to demonstrate to Hilario and the others in the community that livestock farming was not a viable economic solution in the long term, that what was achieved was destroying the forest to plant pastures that only lasted for about 4 years, after which the soil, so poor in nutrients, was exhausted. Furthermore, with so much rain, the cows' footsteps accelerated the process of erosion and deterioration. Likewise, the natives had to take the cattle to the market on foot for up to 2 weeks, during which the animals lost much weight. Hence, they managed to get the intermediaries, who were settlers, to pay very little money for those cattle. However, the promotion made by religious congregations and the Ecuadorian government had been very intense. It was publicized that it was difficult to convince people of the harm of livestock farming in the Amazon forests.

I offered to buy Hilario a bull to feed the workers. Because of the need for money, he accepted. We slaughtered the bull that fed us for three days. The first day was fresh meat; the next two days, it was smoked since we didn't have refrigeration then. To avoid foul odors and insects, I took the skin and the head of the animal in the small canoe, sailed about 20 minutes up the Capahuari River, and dumped these remains about 10 meters away from the water on the shore. The big surprise is that I stopped by there again three days later to collect wood. We found a large number of black-headed vultures (*Coragyps atratus*), red-headed (*Cathartes aura*), and yellow-headed vultures (*Aura sabanera*) in the surrounding trees where we had thrown the remains of the bull, oh surprise! A couple of the King Vultures (*Sarcoramphus papa*) were eating while the Common Vultures waited in the trees. The beauty of these birds was impressive, with their blue and red bald head and white plumage on their neck like condors. It was a bird that was not easily seen, so the natives themselves were impressed by the presence of these birds.

During the construction, I gradually bought all of Hilario's cows, and we always threw away the skin and head as an offering to the King Vultures. These birds were hanging around the project all the time. We eliminated all the cows in the territory. Likewise, this helped me build a great friendship with Hilario that lasts to this day.

The work was progressing; we had built the first structure, the largest cabin that would be the lodge's bar-lobby library, and a double cabin (which housed two rooms). Both structures had only the floor and the roof. There were no walls or bathrooms. I moved to the double cabin where I installed my room, office, and work table for the architect and master carpenter, Rafael. At 5 in the afternoon, all the workers went to the community, and I was left alone in the lagoon. Those were moments that I cherish with gratitude since, in solitude in the lagoon, I could be with myself in silence and with my dreams of carrying out the most important project of my life. The darkness, the nocturnal sounds of fish feeding in the lagoon, frogs singing, bats, and insects became my companions every night. They accompanied me magically; they made me feel part of that.

The work was titanic regarding the energy it demanded, the collection of wood, leaves, and vines for moorings, fuel logistics, personnel management, purchases of materials and supplies, expense and management reports of CANODROS General Management, documentation of the work, presentation of the work under construction at the international tourism fairs in London, Berlin, Madrid, and at the Latin America Travel Mart, which is held annually in a different Latin American city.

We advanced at a regular and systematic pace without stopping. Everything was done correctly. A lot of work and presence were needed, but everything flowed. We had no accidents with the workers, complaints, or problems with the local leaders or the Achuar Nationality; we were all connected to the project.

When replanting the columns of the elevated walkway that linked the main pier with the lodge, the Salesian Missionary, Father Domingo Botasso, director of the Wasakentsa Mission for decades and until today, visited us. A man wholly dedicated to his pastoral work, living with and accompanying the indigenous people for more than 50 years, and witnessing the process of the Achuar people since their incorporation into the system in the 1960s. When he saw the work in that state, he was moved and told me that I was crazy and that I was never going to achieve it, but that he recognized the effort I put into it. I always remember that observation, made with the best goodwill and judgment. He revisited us a year after finishing the work and operating with tourists. We remembered that comment...he apologized for not having "seen" that the intention was so solid and real that the difficulties were overcome and the objective was achieved. Father Domingo became a dear and esteemed friend whom I respect and admire for his integrity and commitment to the Achuar people and his pastoral and missionary work. We shared many annual Assemblies of the Achuar; he always supported my management with his balanced and positive comments, both in Kapawi and in the Achuar air service AEROTSENTSAK, when I presented my reports at the Assemblies.

About 23 months of construction had passed, and we had lived with 90 workers, Achuar, 6 Cuenca workers, the communities of

Kapawi (Amuntai), Sharamentsa, Wayusentsa, and the newborn Wachirpas.

In December 1995, the military detachments on the border with Peru were put on alert due to specific mobilizations in the area. The sergeant commander of the Captain Chiriboga detachment, located in front of the mouth of the Capahuari River where Kapawi is, urgently asked us to lend him a motor canoe to mobilize an armed group that was going to bring some Peruvian soldiers, prisoners, captured infiltrated in our territory. We lent the canoe with an outboard motor and enough fuel, and our soldiers went and brought the prisoners who had been evacuated by helicopter from Cap. Chiriboga to the Amazonas Brigade in Shell. A few days after this event, war was declared with Peru, known as the "Cenepa War." The entire border was declared a war zone. Hence, the army visited us and requested our collaboration with the national emergency. We were forced to deliver five canoes with outboard motors, the entire inventory of canned food, mainly, and the entire reserve of gasoline and diesel. We had to pay the workers before the end of the month, who abandoned the work and returned to their communities, which were involved in the war zone on the border, with the aggravating factor that their Achuar relatives in Peruvian territory were recruited as soldiers to attack Ecuador. The same situation occurred in Ecuador with the group of elite indigenous soldiers known as Iwias (demons). All the workers abandoned work, including the Cuenca residents who had to walk through the jungle to Taisha for 5 days to return to Cuenca via Macas.

Military actions continued intensely until the end of February 1995, and the work was paralyzed until March. It took us a lot of effort to have indigenous workers again. Most of them stayed in their communities, recovering normality after the armed confrontation between relatives and friends, as well as guaranteeing the survival of their families.

We were forced to hire mestizo carpenters domiciled in Shell, Mera, and Puyo to come and work on the finishes: doors, windows, plumbing, and electricity. We also hired Quichua indigenous people from Montalvo and Boberas on the Bobonaza River, who proved to be excellent workers. I remember that when the first Quichuas arrived, it was Sunday, and we were at the port of the Kapawi community with the Achuar workers. When they began to disembark, one of the Achuar workers recognized a Quichua man as the son of the warrior who had killed his grandfather, which irritated him extremely, demanding that we not allow him to stay in Kapawi. The reaction was so violent and severe that we had to ask the Quichua to return to his community.

Our presence in the territory represented a new possibility for the communities, so we began to receive a series of social requests permanently: emergency flights for the seriously ill and snakebitten, uniforms for the school sports teams, supplies and materials for children, trophies for sports championships, payment of salaries to indigenous teachers (without a contract with the country's public education system) in community schools, among others.

This situation distorted the model of the Kapawi Ecolodge project, which consisted of the Achuar learning to manage, administer, and operate tourism in their territory with a first-rate infrastructure. It was not the traditional model of good white people helping poor indigenous people. It was "a business" between the Achuar Nation and the private company CANODROS SA. Therefore, all the pressure of social requests deformed the proposed model.

I called my friend John Perkins and told him my concern, asking him if he had any ideas to somehow solve the issue of the social needs of the communities surrounding the project. From the beginning, John understood very well since I had shared my intention and commitment to make Kapawi Ecolodge in the Achuar territory. A few months later, he called me to tell me that he had a group of friends who were interested in taking a trip to the project and learning more about Kapawi's proposal, which was a new model of private association between an Indigenous Organization and a private tourism Corporation as a conservation tool of the Amazon forest. I was so happy with the news that we prepared the details of the trip; there were 12 people, including John, in addition to Juan Gabriel Carrasco, who was my partner in Ecotrek, with whom we had worked for several years with John and his Dream Change groups, doing Shamanic learning trips.

The visit of this group in the summer of 1995 was something memorable due to the consequences that would be generated in the future, so it seems essential and fair to me to name each one of them:

Bill and Lynne Twist; Jim Gollin; Dave Ellis; Ella Allford; Bob and Wendy Graham; Trish Waldron; Josh Mailman; Deb Emmershien; John Perkins and his 12-year-old daughter Jessica. The group was formed between the contacts of Lynne Twist and John. Some are involved in philanthropic activities, others in Conservation issues, and others are business people. For Lynn, the trip had a particular connotation since, during a previous shamanic experience in Africa, she had a vision of some indigenous faces painted red with feather arrangements on their heads. This vision was recurring in Lynne, so John related those visions to the Achuar in the Ecuadorian Amazon.

This was a very entertaining and exciting group. There was a lot of joy, good jokes, conversations, and profound reflections on the world situation on issues mainly related to social justice, conservation, and ontology.

When this group arrived in Kapawi, there was only the roof and floor of the large Bar-Lobby cabin, two latrines in the forest, and the construction site at its maximum intensity, with work everywhere and collecting wood and leaves. Luchito Peñafiel, who cooked for the workers, was in charge of feeding the group. When the purpose and intention of this work were shared with them, they felt identified with the concept. They were pleased that it was an innovative proposal for the time, based on the goodwill of the apparently antagonistic parties, such as Indigenous organizations and capitalist corporations.

The model involved creating a business in the indigenous territory and allowing them to learn to manage and operate tourism over a 15-

year learning curve. In the long term, the ownership and management of the operating company would be transferred to the Indigenous Organization for self-management. At the same time, it would contribute to rescuing the traditions of the Achuar culture and mainly to conserving the Amazon Tropical Forest.

They were the first foreign visitors to appear in the area, so their presence aroused curiosity in the communities we visited and the construction workers. For visitors, it was the privilege of experiencing the wonders of the Amazon in a pristine state. It was the opportunity to execute the protocols I had designed for the lodge's operation regarding community visits, walks in the forest, and river navigation. However, we lacked the necessary equipment at that time.

The diversity of trails and Amazonian ecosystems in the area of influence of the Lodge, navigation on large rivers such as the Pastaza, medium ones such as the Capahuari, Ishpingo and small ones such as the Kuzutkau, visits to the communities and cultural exchange, offered the visitors an excellent opportunity to learn about the biodiversity and beauty of the Amazon, its people and feel the importance of its Conservation. All these moments and experiences were consolidated in the visit to the "Uwijin" (Shaman) Rafael Taish, in the Wayusentsa community, where the group was offered the option of experiencing the medicine or power plant of Natem (Ayahuasca in Achuar – *Banisteriopsis caapi*). On this occasion, when the group asked Rafael what they could do to help the Achuar, Rafael Taish said there was no need if they just wanted to come to help. Still, if they tried to free themselves with the Achuar, they would have to work to change the dream of the modern world, which impacts and threatens the Jungle and Nature worldwide.

Some people had experienced Ayahuasca before, but for most, it was a new experience. Each of those who took it had a profoundly personal experience, with visions and physical sensations, which transported them to a moment and space of "truth" to "see" their own lives from a perspective in which the mind and ego do not. They are actors. It was more of a "feel" truth. The clarity and meaning manifested in some of them in the following days and weeks. Still, the encounter with that sacred space remained impregnated in their lives.

We flew to civilization again and visited the FINAE leaders whom the group wanted to meet. Likewise, the Achuar leaders wished to ask the visitors what they thought of the experience in their territory and how they saw the project's future.

We arrived at the OINAE office. It was a small room on the ground floor with a table with two chairs, a typewriter, and a half bathroom under a staircase from the apartment on the upper floor. A head of bananas hung from a beam of the ceiling, and on the floor in a corner, an old mattress... But on the walls of the little room, there were papers posted with the projects they were looking to achieve for their nascent organization. In these excellent papers, the vision of the Achuar people was represented: Health, Education, Organizational Strengthening, Communications, Territory, Alternative Economic Development, and Air Service. On each project flipchart, they developed the strategy to achieve the goals. In health, education, and territory, they had to relate to the Ecuadorian State and others with the State, Foundations, NGOs, and Universities. They had a clear vision.

Seeing this, the group's friends were absorbed in understanding the scope of the Achuar people's vision and that, as a first step, they had completed the alternative economic development and conservation project KAPAWI ECOLODGE. They exchanged comments, explanations, suggestions, and words of appreciation. We were all happy with this exchange, having been the Achuar's confidants who shared their vision with us.

We ascended the Andes mountain range in our van to the small and picturesque town of Baños, at the foot of the Tungurahua volcano, known for its hot springs. We stayed at the Sangay Hotel, had dinner together, and then met at the bar; we were all delighted, excited, and eager to continue enjoying what we had experienced before arriving at the noisy civilization in Quito the next day. We ordered some drinks and beers and began to remember the trip, from the contact made by John and Lynne in the USA to day by day with all its particularities, always with good humor. In a moment of calm, someone asked…after meeting the Achuar and their Kapawi Lodge project, after they shared their vision and projects with us, were we as a group going to do something? Will we contribute with that energy and intention that is so clear and powerful? After a short silence, one of them offered $10,000 to contribute to the distribution over three years; after a while, someone else said it was reasonable and committed to the same, and another and another and another joined the same commitment. Suddenly, we had committed $110,000, divided over 3 years, to show solidarity with the Achuar. They sent $33,000 per year plus $10,000 at the beginning for the Achuar to initiate a Master Plan for their territory.

Just like that, for three years, without asking how they will use the money or asking for accountability, nothing... we simply hand over the money, and the Achuar leaders will know how to manage and what to do. Trust and supportive support!

The construction of Kapawi continued without significant developments; in the carpentry, we built all the furniture for the rooms, restaurant, and bar. We hired the Ecuadorian Air Force to charter the Casa C-295 aircraft for a flight from Quito to Montalvo on the banks of the Bobonaza River. The cargo flight included 50 mattresses, all the plumbing for phytosanitary installation, toilets, sinks, refrigerators, freezers, and 10,000-liter tanks for water storage. There was nowhere to put a pin on that plane. In Montalvo, the large canoes used in the construction were waiting for us. The commander of the Montalvo military Battalion, upon learning about Kapawi, graciously provided us with personnel to unload the plane and take the cargo to the boats. He also invited us to dinner and offered us lodging to continue our river trip the next day, taking all this equipment along the Bobonaza River to its mouth in the Pastaza River, which we crossed to the mouth of the Capahuari River to finally reach Kapawi.

Kapawi Ecolodge opened its operations to the public in July 1996. It was an icon in the international market, built without using a single nail; it was the first photovoltaic installation with a capacity of 9 Kilowatts. Likewise, it brought the country the first 4-stroke outboard engines with low environmental impact and the first ecotourism project resulting from an alliance between an Indigenous organization and private companies.

It has been an exemplary operation, a model of good practices, and has received several recognitions, including 1998 Tourism for Tomorrow, British Airways; 2000 Ecotourism Excellence Award, Conservation International; 2002 Ecotourism Award, Skal International; 2004 – Conservation Category – Sustainable Tourism Award for Conservation (STAC) (third place); 2009 – PRODUCT Awarded Top 50 Ecolodges 2009 by the Editors of National Geographic Adventure Magazine.

Bill and Lynne Twist returned to Kapawi in January 1996 with the first group of visitors. Although Kapawi was not officially open, we welcomed them, and they enjoyed the services, excursions, and interaction with communities. Likewise, upon returning to the USA, this group contributed $35,000 US for the Mapping Project with community participation, which the Achuar had started with the donation received from the first group.

In 1992, some indigenous nationalities of the Amazon received property titles to community lands in their ancestral territories. The Achuar needed the titles to coincide with the territories and their actual use. The community-mapping project required communities to first make a map, highlighting the geographical features they have customarily considered their boundaries, comparing them with title boundaries, defining differences, and seeking solutions with neighboring communities. This was the first project that The Pachamama Alliance officially carried out with the Achuar.

The success of the first two groups and the relationship CANODROS (Kapawi) with the OINAE (Interprovincial Organization of the Achuar Nationality of Ecuador) inspired the Twists and those who visited us to start The Pachamama Alliance (www.pachamama.org) in 1996. The fluidity of the relationship with the Achuar required starting the Pachamama Foundation in Ecuador as a local counterpart, which executed the programs and projects being implemented. I was its ad honorem president from its constitution until 2014. Cristina Santa Cruz was the first executive director of Fundación Pachamama. Belén Páez replaced her in 1997 when Cristina went to study for her master's degree at Cornell University in the USA. From the opening of Kapawi, Bill came to Ecuador every 3 or 4 months, bringing a new group of contributors or simply working with Cristina and Belén to implement the projects developed in the Achuar territory. Likewise, about 40 HF radios allowed daily communication between the communities and with the organization's offices in Puyo.

The Achuar had achieved a lot of progress. They had agreements with the Ministries of Health and Education. They had implemented a bicultural, bilingual education system in the community schools, with some indigenous teachers from the public system. They also implemented a system of health promoters who were trained in nursing and tropical diseases in some communities. They were following a process to expand coverage.

The management capacity of the Achuar leaders was admirable, as was the commitment and attitude of getting involved in the system of Western Ecuadorian and global culture. This presence of the Achuar inspired Bill and Lynne Twist to establish the responsibility to support the Achuar in their search for a space in the world, maintaining their identity and self-determination as a people. In those years, the threat of the expansion of the oil frontier in the Ecuadorian Amazon was already felt, which was filtered by the bad experience in the provinces of Napo and Orellana with TEXACO and the negative impact on the well-being of the Cofan and Huaoranis peoples. It was already seen as a great problem for the survival of the people and the Amazon forests and rivers in the south-central area.

That was the beginning of an incredible relationship between the Pachamama Foundation and the Achuar Nation, initially, and other Amazonian Nationalities from Ecuador, Colombia, Peru, and Bolivia.

The Achuar have had in TPA and Fundación Pachamama one of their strongest and most permanent allies, who have supported them in all aspects of the organization and in a very particular way, for example, by allocating funds to pay the salary of Achuar leaders while they live in Puyo. That way, the leaders would not face the stress of living in the city and paying for everything, which, in other cases, would have allowed indigenous leaders to be bribed and corrupted by oil or logging companies.

Organizational strengthening, training, and legal and juridical support are the areas where we mainly collaborate with other programs that receive permanent attention, such as "Jungle Mamas" (Ikiama Nukuri, which means Women guardians of the forest), for midwives who protect pregnant mothers and children from birth to their first year of life. It has been very successful in its specific objectives. It has provided an additional benefit: giving a stronger voice to Achuar women in all aspects of life, including families and communities.

The other iconic projects in which Pachamama has collaborated magnificently are Kapawi Ecolodge, which has supported the Achuar in their management since it was transferred by CANODROS, and AEROTSENTSAK, the Achuar air service that operated successfully and that received from TPA a twin-engine Islander aircraft with capacity for nine passengers plus the pilot.

Pachamama's relationship with the Achuar Nation has existed since 1997 and has been profoundly effective in helping the voice of the Amazonian indigenous people be heard and supporting the defense and conservation of the territory. On the other hand, it has created an authentic space for people in the modern world to find a noble cause to support and contribute, with an environmentally sustainable human presence that is spiritually satisfying and socially just.

The commercial strategy of CANODROS SA was to offer its Galapagos Explorer cruise in the Galapagos Islands, together with Kapawi Ecolodge in the Amazon. Thus, we presented our offer at the international tourism fairs at ITB Berlin, World Travel Market London, America Travel Mart; the market expected...However, a major unforeseen event occurred. In January 1996, the Galapagos Explorer cruise ship sank, fortunately without personal misfortunes. However, the vessel was lost entirely, a hard blow for the company. Kapawi opened to the public in July 1996, five and a half months after the shipwreck. We went to the market without planned commercial support. However, Kapawi had aroused interest in the international market, so it had a very auspicious opening, becoming a star product for the following years.

CANODROS took 2 years to replace the vessel with a beautiful ship of 4077 Gross Tons, 89 meters long, with a cruising speed of 17 knots and a capacity for 100 passengers in 50 luxury suites operated in the Greek islands. The Galapagos Explorer II (GEII) has been operating since February 1998 and partially recovered its pre-accident market share over the following 4 years, including a 2-month shutdown due to a major failure in the propulsion system. Kapawi worked very well with satisfied customers and received excellent comments. Hence, the company's general management asked me to contribute to the ship's operation to enhance its competitiveness and occupancy.

Daniel Koupermann C.

Photos of the Amazon Rainforest:

1. Father Bolla (Yankuam) and Daniel

2. Father Bolla (Yankuam) with an Achuar child

3. Father Raúl Etsa in Miazal

4. Elder Tukupi weaving a chankina

5. Kapawi Lodge at its beginning

6. Kapawi Lodge, aerial view

7. Elder Tukupi preparing a blowgun dart

8. Carlos Pérez crossing the river

9. Don Carlos Pérez dreaming

10. Crossing the Tsurim River, Miazal

11. Daniel with Carlos Pérez, Rafael, and María Elena Lecaro

12. Log foundation during the construction of the Sharamentsa airstrip

13. An anaconda found at Kapawi Lodge

14. Paiche fishing with Juan Baca and Marcelino Tukupi, 1982

15. Father Raúl and Daniel in Miazal

8. GEII – Mn/ Galapagos Explorer II – Galapagos Islands

The proposal was a refreshing challenge after the effort and energy put into Kapawi. The opportunity to contribute to the ship's operation in the Enchanted Islands was different and exciting. The idea was to make the cruise operation a model of good practices in one of the most important natural sanctuaries on the planet.

We characterized the atmosphere inside the ship, changing all the pictures in hallways and cabins from Greek temples and gods to photos and paintings of the Galapagos Islands' fauna, flora, and landscapes.

Based on the experience of Kapawi Lodge, we also developed a 40-page booklet about the islands and the boat on recycled paper that was delivered to each cabin. It had detailed information on the evolutionary processes in the Galapagos with maps and details of each place of visit in the National Park, with a checklist of species, so that the passengers could record their sightings, a chronology of the human history of the Galapagos, and unprecedented informative material, which was also delivered to Tour Operators and Travel Agents at international fairs. Other operators in the Galapagos and the Amazon emulated this type of material.

The quality of the guides' keynote lectures and daily briefings was notably improved, and the best expedition leaders were hired, such as Felipe Degel, Salvador Cazar, and Ma. Gabriela Espinoza and Etienne de Backer, who trained the guides with less experience, formed a team of excellent naturalist guides, improving the passengers' experience. We changed all the exterior lights of the boat to anti-insect lights to avoid attracting and transporting insects from one island to another. We converted the Casino into the Naturalist's Room, where abundant material on the islands' natural history was available to passengers, microscopes to observe tissues of species, inventories, and studies from the Charles Darwin Scientific Station. We agreed with the Scientific Station to occasionally have a scientist on board to monitor indicators of water acidity, oxygen, and mineral concentrations, marking of animals at visiting sites, echolocation, etc.

We replaced the fiberglass boats used to transport passengers from the ship to the islands with Zodiacs with a capacity for 18 people and 4-stroke outboard engines. We also installed ozone stations in the water pipe circuit, especially in the sewage treatment plant's ocean discharge, to minimize chlorine discharge into the sea.

The human team of the GEII hotel department achieved the highest service standards. Their professionalism and empowerment allowed us to systematically achieve high customer satisfaction. For several years, we obtained excellent ratings and reviews in the CLIA (Cruise Lines International Association) ranking.

The other key aspect was to improve the itinerary, incorporating the west coast of Isabela Island, with a visit to Fernandina Island, Bolívar Channel, an area in which the youngest lands of the archipelago exist, and where whale watching is feasible almost all year round. By doing this, the opportunity was given to incorporate an essential content of social responsibility in the operation of the cruise, since one of the permanent complaints of the island communities is that the operation of large ships does not benefit the local population.

We got the Galapagos National Park to authorize the change; we anchored in Puerto Villamil (Isabela Island) so the passengers could spend the entire day on land. The visiting options were very diverse and exciting: Trails and hidden beaches in Las Diablas; hikes to the crater of the Sierra Negra Volcano (7.2 x 9.3 km), the second largest volcanic crater in the world after the crater of the Ngorongoro Volcano (16 x 19 km) in northern Tanzania. Also, snorkeling in the pools of the fishermen's pier, the Tintoreras islet to observe marine iguanas and sharks, or simply tour the town, seeing the islanders' daily life and enjoying the port's beautiful beaches.

We trained five local restaurants in menu design, preparation, and food management. We advised them on some physical improvements, especially in the kitchen and bathrooms. An average of 20 passengers had lunch at each restaurant. We agreed with the fishermen's cooperative that they would provide white fish every week the boat arrived in Isabela, which worked well for some weeks and not others. It was difficult for them to commit regularly, but a space was still open for them to contribute.

There were no tourist buses in the town then, so we trained and gave GEII polo shirts to the owners of taxi vans. We hired up to 20 vans for the entire day to transport passengers to the different activities. It was an exceptional experience to be the first large tourist boat to regularly arrive in Puerto Villamil and contribute directly to the local economy.

The operation was carried out successfully. The passengers appreciated this visit and its social content. The community was satisfied and hopeful of Isabela's great opportunity to show its responsible tourism vocation. Four months after visiting Isabela, the National Government and the Navy imposed limitations and controls on illegal sea cucumber fishing, which endangered the survival of this species. Unfortunately, the prices paid by Korean and Chinese merchants were so high that they encouraged illegal fishing.

As a reaction against the government's restrictive measures, these illegal fishermen planned to make a show of force, kidnapping the passengers of the GEII, preventing them from returning on board after the all-day visit. Fortunately, a local collaborator let us know 3 days before these malevolent intentions, so we canceled the boat's visit to Puerto Villamil, keeping navigation on the west coast of Isabela on the itinerary. A great opportunity was lost due to the decision of a powerful group that only saw its interests rather than those of the vast majority of the community. The same story that has been repeated in humanity for millennia.

In November 2002, Don Carlos Pérez died, and his children succeeded him in administering the companies. They found irregularities in CANODROS's General Management, so they replaced the General Manager with a well-known group executive. This executive had a reputation for having an iron fist and managed the corporation's insurance area for years.

It was a great surprise for me that the dismissed Manager, to whom I had been his right-hand man, trusted man, advisor, and friend, left the company without communicating with me or telling me anything. He simply disappeared, and he did not answer my calls and messages. I never knew the reasons why he was dismissed. I imagine that he committed ethical and/or administrative offenses.

Faced with such a strange situation, and because I had been their trusted man, the new administration thought I knew of these irregularities, so I decided to stay in the position to demonstrate that I had no knowledge. Audits were carried out for an uninterrupted year, making it clear that I had no connection with the irregular management decisions other than in operational, strategic, marketing, and customer service matters.

The new Manager had great animosity towards me, almost from the beginning of his management. He asked me to try to fire the hotel workers of the ship, who had been working for the company for a long time, due to the high cost and risk of the employer's retirement. I had invested so much effort in creating an excellent team; we had achieved high functionality and efficiency, and he asked me to replace it with new staff. Logically, I refused, which made the Manager very upset.

Here began one of my life's most complex, intense, and challenging periods. I experienced humility as a virtue and the most genuine and authentic attitude to see and know oneself. Humility comes from helplessness, the impossibility of reacting reasonably and enduring bad intentions, aggression, and simply accepting and showing dignity and integrity. The new General Manager did everything possible to make me resign; he removed my jurisdiction and functions. However, my feelings became a personal challenge, a demonstration of strength that I decided to respond to, which took me to the limit of my creativity and work capabilities. When we first met on a trip to Berlin to the ITB fair, upon returning, we had a night in Madrid; he asked me what I was going to do. I told him I would buy a Barcelona soccer team shirt for my youngest son and then go to the Espasa Calpe bookstore to buy some books. He asked me to accompany him, so we went around together. Arriving at the bookstore, each went their own way, with the agreement to meet at the checkout in an hour. When we met I saw that he had a book with a cover of 2 solid colors, when I asked him about the book he showed it to me, it was "The 48 Laws of Power" by Robert Green, based on the statements of the work of The Prince by Nicolás Machiavelli, Sun Tzu, Clausewitz, Bismark, Talleyrand, Casanova and other strategists, statesmen, courtiers, seducers and swindlers. Without giving me so much detail, he recommended the book to me, telling me that he was replacing it since it was a bedside book for him. I was tempted and bought the book. I started reading it, and it aroused great interest in me because of how well conceived, clearly explained, and applied with real-life examples, the management of these laws to have and maintain power at the expense of others or opportunities. When he began to harass me, I understood that I had an enemy in him who sought to harm me. The laws of power helped me have the appropriate weapons and strategies to endure and maintain my integrity. Life...

We had begun the process of creating the standard recipe for food service to guests and crew in my department, intending to control the cost and the quality standard; it was a meticulous job, organizing hundreds of items, carrying out tests with the chefs on board, in short, an incredibly complex job. We developed it in Excel so well that a specialized firm was hired to work with me to transfer the work from Excel to Windows and create software. Seeing the usefulness of the job done with so many collaborators, including my colleague, was satisfying. Freddy Espinel was my right hand in administrative and operational work at the GEII.

One of the unforgettable moments was when the Manager asked me if I had the inventory of hotel supplies, food, and beverages up to date. I told him that in the established procedure, at each end of the cruise (twice a week), the Resident Manager on board sent us a disk with the discharges and deposits and a list of orders for the next cruise.

Then, he told me that he had given the order that they should no longer send me the list from the ship and that I, from the central office in Guayaquil, should be able to replenish the vessel with the hundreds of items that were consumed, sent fresh and urgent food to the Galapagos by air, and the rest by sea, in a journey of 3 to 4 days.

It was nonsense at first, but on the other hand, it was a job in which I was exposed to failure due to its difficulty, the volume of the procedure, and the factors that I did not control, which affected the achievement of results. I drew strength from the depths of my convictions, stayed working until late at night, and succeeded. I sent the replacement items on board without needing the ship's list.

The Manager recognized the work, but it was useless since he had said in the Board of Directors that he would make me resign and that, for any eventuality, within two years, he would terminate my employment.

That's how it was; after two years, he called me to his office, and in a satirical way, he literally told me that, much to his regret, he asked me to leave the company and that he had ordered human talent to liquidate my salary for untimely dismissal. I slammed my hand hard on his desk, which startled him. I asked him why he had taken so long to dismiss me, that he could have done it sooner and avoided so many bad moments and abuses of authority. He told me he wanted to give himself the pleasure of making me resign; he tried to give himself the pleasure of breaking me... I then said to him that he must recognize that he failed, that he had to use all his power to hurt me for 2 years and could not, and that my integrity was untouched. I asked him why he was such a bad person, why he was so screwed up, and his response was: *since that's the way things have gone well for me, therefore, why should I change?* I thanked him for having forcefully taught me what one should not be. I learned so much in those days that I recognize that this Manager who mistreated me and offended me in word and deed has been a teacher during my training as an administrator. Those 2 years of my life of so much suffering and stress contributed significantly to my professional training and to my humanity.

In developing these situations, I tried to communicate with the children of Don Carlos Pérez, with whom I had developed a friendship, talked, and established personal contact. They were the current owners, and I wanted to tell them what was happening and try to find a solution, an adequate exit, without so much abuse. They never attended to me or answered my messages. They left me completely defenseless during the two years of harassment.

How much disappointment, frustration, anger, emptiness, anguish, and sadness I felt when I saw that my 15 years of work, commitment, dedication, sacrifice, loyalty, passion, and creativity were not recognized and appreciated by the bosses. However, I am sure coworkers in Kapawi and the GEII, clients, business allies, indigenous communities, and academia recognized and appreciated what was achieved.

Kapawi has been "the project" of my life; I was so fortunate to find a person who was inspired by an idea and trusted me to carry it out, who allowed me to find a space with my deepest aspirations, beliefs, principles, and commitments. A space where I could put into action everything conceived in theory, where I had to practice values such as reciprocity, conscious effort, and voluntary suffering, sacrifice, and receive the benefits of deep personal satisfaction to have the appreciation of others, to receive grace, to be deeply connected to the force of nature, and to achieve goals. Kapawi is my altar and place of one of my most representative offerings to life.

9. Transition

When I left CANODROS, I had a very intense feeling of emptiness, incredible frustration, and sadness at having given so much effort and commitment and having ended up in such an inconsequential way. Now it was time to look for something to do, to generate money again, and to be able to support my family. I should research the popular festivals in Ecuador, organize different trips, and be able to enter the market with something innovative. I agreed with my friend Alfredo Pastor, a professional photographer, to accompany me in this investigation and document photographically to make a good archive for him and for use in marketing for my initiative. We traveled the country for 10 months almost uninterruptedly, visiting places where they celebrated some festivity, or in many cases just visiting the places, talking with Priests in charge of the churches, or with the elderly people of the town, in stores, parks, parish meetings, political holdings, etc. I collected fascinating information about the Catholic festive calendar, many of whose celebrations coincide with the ancestral Indigenous festivities of the solstices and equinoxes or about the remembrance of apparitions of the Virgin Mary, her miracles, or incredible stories of magical realism, like that of the lady who took care of the image of the Lord of the Earthquake in Patate, province of Tungurahua. She was consecrated to the church service when she was fifteen years old, and her job was to dress the life-size image of the Lord of the Earthquake in a different dress every week.

This image has enough dresses with brocades and gold and silver threads to use for several years. The lady attended us and took us to the trousseau and the image. A lady who generated a lot of peace and presence with this sacred work to which she dedicated her entire life.

In contrast, in the history of the "Las Diabladas" festival in Pìllaro, a neighboring town, the story is that once a year, from January 1 to 6, the devils have vacations and go out of their world to be with and bother humans. There are several interpretations of this event and its origins in the haciendas of the colonial era. The design of the devil masks used for the festival from January 1 to 6 is spectacular. They give anonymity to the people who use them, who dance and make people dance, along with other characters such as the Guaricha, which represents a woman with a doll, which represents the child, and who, dancing non-stop, screams in search of the baby's father. It is a party without any religious meaning where people are freed from the protocols of routine life. And they are pleased.

When we went to Ingapirca (Inca archaeological ruins) for the "Inti Raymi," the June Solstice that brings together indigenous people from many Cañar communities and visitors in general, we were walking and taking photos of the people and their activities, when we found a circle of Yachaks (Shamans), who had gathered to do a joint ceremony of gratitude. Seeing the back of a white man with very long hair and clothing caught my attention; he was different from most Indigenous people in the circle. We stayed at that angle of vision until the ceremony was over, when this white man with long hair and a beard suddenly turned and walked towards us. When he passed by, I recognized him and called him Alejandro... he looked me in the eyes, and then eye contact spoke to me...Daniel, it was Alejo Valdivieso, an old friend from youth with whom we had shared time and unforgettable experiences, like when we went to hunt turtledoves in the barley field of his father's Shuracpamba farm, where we had to walk from the main road down the mountain for 4 hours, until reaching the Hacienda, a fascinating place completely isolated from everything. I was surprised to see him transformed into a Yachak and become part of a select group of old Shamans from different parts of Ecuador, Peru, and Colombia. It was a lovely reunion after 30 years of not seeing each other.

The story of "Taita" Alejandro is interesting: Upon the death of his father, he received the Shuralpampa hacienda as an inheritance, which soon stopped producing since it stopped raining for years, all the water sources dried up so that Alejandro was never able to continue with the agricultural work of the Hacienda and due to the isolation of the place it was not possible to access any source of water. He abandoned the farm and let time and vegetation invade the house and facilities. One day, a group in Cuenca invited a Mexican Shaman known as one of the "Red Path" teachers of the Nahuatl-Lakota-Sioux tradition. They were looking for a spiritual teaching. The Shaman asked them to choose an isolated place to do his ceremonies, away from all distractions. Alejandro offered his abandoned place. When they went to see it, it seemed to the Shaman to be the perfect place, so they cleaned the undergrowth and the area around the house. The Hacienda was the site of the first ceremony; what was strange and extraordinary was that the next day, it rained... and in the following days of the ceremony, the water springs gushed again. Alejandro couldn't believe it since it was like a miracle after so many years without rain. From that moment on, Alejandro began on the Red Path. The "miracle" that occurred, the Shaman interpreted as a sign for the place and the person to be chosen as a ceremonial site, with a sacred fire that they started and has remained uninterrupted burning for more than 30 years. In Shuracpamba, Temazcal ceremonies and vision quests are offered to this day.

Researching the popular festivals of Ecuador took me a year, a pleasant experience that allowed me to tour my country and learn about its most representative traditions. The collected material is the draft of a Calendar of Popular Festivals of Ecuador, which rests in my computer's memory.

10. Aerotsentsak

I was invited by The Pachamama Alliance to contribute to the project to support the Achuar air service, the same one that had already existed for about 5 years. When I arrived, they operated a Cessna 172 light plane for a pilot and three passengers or 700 pounds, a Cessna 182 for a pilot and three passengers or 800 lbs., and a Cessna 206 small plane for a pilot and five passengers or 1000 pounds. Non-indigenous administrators, who had difficulties achieving self-sufficiency, managed the air service. Likewise, the Achuar leadership used it to cover organizational needs. The needs did not cover the cost of the flights they used.

They hired me for a 2-year consultancy as the Achuar Air Service manager. On a personal level, it was an exciting challenge. I knew the environment of air services in the Amazon, having been a permanent user for more than 30 years. I knew the importance of air service for the communities and families inside the jungle, their only means of communication with the outside world. And my fascination with small planes, airplanes, and fantastic flying machines.

We designed and operated a new administrative and operating system with Bill Twist. Initially, making a diagnosis of the situation, gathering as much data as possible from previous operations, about which there was almost no information. The Air Service was behind on legal benefits with the IESS and SRI. It had been paying for fuel and salaries with contributions from the Pachamama Foundation. It had no reserves for overhauling engines and propellers. It took about 6 months to get the house in order and start running the airline operation with self-sufficient cash flow. With the support of Pachamama Alliance and Wings of Hope, we managed to stabilize the operation, make the necessary overhauls, and obtain a stock of parts and spare parts.

It was fascinating for me to learn about the world of aviation, global regulations, manufacturers' procedures, updating bulletins and regulations, supply of spare parts, and operation manuals; I enjoyed, became interested, and educated myself on these topics. The underlying objective was to design a system with simple, precise, and efficient procedures so that the Achuar indigenous people themselves could manage their air service, developing learning processes and administrative skills.

Together with the leaders, we named the air service: AEROTSENTSAK, tsentsak in Achuar are the arrows used in the bodoquera or cebatana (blowgun), they are also the invisible arrows, which can be sent in different contexts, for example, when a man falls in love with a woman or vice versa. It is because he fired his tsentsaks that they hit the target. Or when a Shaman sends a "maleo" wrong or sound energy, he does so through tsentsaks, hence the name of the air service.

I developed the essential tools to manage the air service: Accounting plan, Budget, Cash Flow, Bank Book, Rate per plane, and Inventories. We wrote the pilots' Operations Manual for Administration, Flight Planning, and Maintenance. I translated the Operation Manuals of the Cessna 172, 182, and 206 into Spanish and then of the twin-engine Islander. We built a hangar with all the technical specifications, with a contribution from CODEMPE (Council of Nationalities and Peoples of Ecuador), the state organization in charge of indigenous and ancestral peoples' affairs.

The Pachamama Alliance donated a Britten Norman Islander BN-2 twin-engine aircraft with a capacity for a pilot and nine passengers or 2000 lbs of cargo. This aircraft was purchased in Florida for $250,000, flown to Canada to an authorized Britten-Norman workshop, and had some special modifications made for operation in the Amazon for another $300,000. The plane was super-equipped, including two additional windows for tourist use, structural reinforcement, and reinforced landing gear, among other significant modifications. With this donation, we had the most versatile fleet of small planes at the Shell-Río Amazonas station.

We managed an impeccable operation, operating 174 runways in the Achuar, Huaorani, Shuar, Kichwa, Shiwiar, and Sàpara territories. We offered a discounted rate for Indigenous peoples and a commercial rate for individual or institutional clients. I admire the jungle pilots who operate in the Ecuadorian Amazon, where they fly to remote communities with very rudimentary dirt and mud runways and where climatic conditions change in the blink of an eye.

With the proper management of sales and collections and with the opening and positioning of the market, we managed to be self-sufficient and have up-to-date reserves for periodic maintenance of the engines and propellers. We paid salaries on time, were up to date with social benefits and taxes, and maintained fuel reserves for uninterrupted operation.

After a year, when the operation and administration were stabilized entirely, it was time to train an Achuar to be the future administrator of AEROTSENTSAK. The leaders chose Santiago Kawarim, who had been President of the Achuar organization FINAE for two terms. He was a school teacher, a profession acquired by studying in the Wasakentsa and Gualaquiza Missions with the Salesian missionaries. We did critical public relations work, relating the Air Service to NGOs, municipalities, provincial governments, and the Ministry of Health and Education, which expanded our customer base.

Santiago sat next to me for 12 hours daily for an uninterrupted year. Santiago studied to be a teacher, so with that level of education, it was necessary to develop skills and knowledge to be a Business Administrator. He demonstrated aptitude and a great interest in learning to use the tools I had designed. With patience, discipline, and daily practice, little by little, he assimilated the principles of administration and the logic of a businessman. Whenever he faced difficulty in a procedure or concept, he asked questions freely.

A good example was his difficulty differentiating the bankbook from the cash flow. So, to understand, we made analogies with everyday life situations of the Achuar in the jungle. I asked him what he would do if he knew that his wife's relatives were coming to visit him at his house for a week. He had to go hunting and fishing every day or every other day to provide food for the guests. Cash flow is then knowing what day and how much food would come in, and what day and how much food would be used. The bankbook was to understand how much food there was at the end of each day, regardless of when more food would arrive or when food would be available to cook. In this way, the differentiation of these tools and their use in practice was clear. It was a lovely process because of the interest that Santiago showed and because of my desire and commitment to make the management model we proposed work.

My two and a half years in Aerotsentsak allowed me to get to know the Achuar from a different perspective. I worked very closely with the political "power" since the Air Service was a means of satisfying commitments with the bases.

Santiago managed AEROTSENTSAK for two years, and then he was removed by a decision made by the General Assembly of the NAE. Unfortunately, he did not train any indigenous colleagues to replace him as planned. He continued using the tools, which worked very well. Likewise, the reasons for the removal were political, so they chose a person who did not have the profile to carry out the mentioned management, which caused the Air Service to gradually decrease its operational, economic, and financial capacity until reaching bankruptcy. The planes were sold to cover liabilities, labor, leases, IESS, and SRI.

After Aerotsentsak, I began to guide the groups of The Pachamama Alliance again, visiting the Achuar territory in the Ecuadorian Amazon every year. Guiding groups to the Amazon and being the facilitator in their encounter with the beauty and strength of the tropical forest, with the Achuar culture and the ceremonies with Natem "Ayahuasca," has been, for me, a source of learning in a space of service, which has nourished me for so many years and in which I have had the honor and privilege of witnessing incredible personal transformations.

The Amazon rainforest is shown in all its splendor on hikes through the forest trails of Tierra Firme, Igapos, and Varzeas; the navigations on the great Pastaza River and on the Bobonaza, Capahuari, Ishpingo, and Kuzutkau rivers, the lagoons, swamps and meanders, the Achuar communities and families in their routine life, the drinking of guayusa tea (*Ilex guayusa*) in the early mornings, where dreams are shared and interpreted, family stories, wars, memories of trips or experiences are heard, sharing the atmosphere of daily life waking up with chickens, hens, children crying, laughing, carrying water, their farms, crafts, customs, and traditions; their vision of life and the world and especially, control and self-sufficiency at a personal and family level, protected in a life where the hierarchy is community life, where individual or family will and interests are submitted to the interests, needs and community decisions.

On these trips, travelers are invited to focus on the fact that the trip is a pilgrimage of learning and searching for clarity, healing, understanding of our experience in life, and the meaning and intention that each one can give to life itself. The travelers expose their vulnerability and humanity, which I can see for myself and the group members. The learning and experience are individual and personal. Still, they occur in a group context, and that is what makes each group unique. It also establishes a temporary but intimate relationship between the members.

11. Guatemala and the Mayas

When my wife Linda and I visited San Francisco in January 2012, we were invited to a dinner at Bill and Lynne Twist's house, where John Perkins and his wife Kiman were also present. We talked about the rumors of the end of the world due to the end of the "Long Count" of the Mayan calendar, which would occur on the solstice of December 21, 2012.

The Long Count is one of several calendars that the Mayas developed. It includes five time cycles of 5,125.36 years (13 Baktuns of 394.25 years each). The complete "Long Count" time is 25,626.8 years, which is very close to the 25,767 years of the **Precession movement of the Earth's equinoxes**.

On December 21, 2012, the last of the five cycles of 5,125.36 years was completed. The beginning of the first fifth of a new complete cycle metaphysically implies a new "time" where fundamental changes in the behavior of humanity will manifest. It will be a time in which the qualities of coexistence will be elevated, where there will be more equity, where the value of power will be replaced little by little by solidarity, and human selfishness and misery will subside. The beginning of a new era of 25,626.8 years!! That was the context for the conversation about possibly taking trips together again. The last time we took a trip together was in 1993, 18 years before (2012).

The Mayas and their calendars, their gigantic cities abandoned and invaded by the jungle, fire ceremonies, the beginning of a new era... There were so many exciting components that immediately aroused our enthusiasm. We knew we would have enough passengers between his and my contacts to make a viable group. John had been to Guatemala a few years ago, where he met Julio Tot, his guide. He gave me his contact information, so I called and arranged a meeting with Julio in Flores, Guatemalan Petén. Julio was a guide specializing in Mayan Culture, History, and Archaeology, a native of Petén, and involved with Mayan archeology since he was a child, since his father was one of the first local assistants to the archaeologists of the University of Pennsylvania from 1956 to 1969.

I also contacted a Mayan Quiché spiritual leader from Alta Verapaz through an NGO that sponsored the celebration of a meeting between Mayan spiritual leaders since the end of the civil war (1960-1996) because one of the axes of the treaty of peace that they signed, was to allow the indigenous Mayans to use their sacred sites for their ceremonies in their daily lives. When we met Tata Domingo, Julio had little contact with Mayan spirituality or traditional shamanic practices.

Once I did the exploration and met Julio and Tata Domingo, we organized the first trip to Guatemala, promoting it through John's website and our contact list. It was a surprise! We had 35 people, plus John and me. Julio was inspired and gave a masterful guide on Mayan and Guatemalan history and archeology, including his vision and testimony of what he experienced during the war years. Tata Domingo officiated fire ceremonies, which deeply captivated everyone with his presence and Julio's translation, which, due to his knowledge of the Mayan Quiche language and English, transmitted what Tata Domingo said with the perfect emotional and philosophical meaning.

With his psycho-navigation ceremonies accompanied by drum rhythms and his conversations about knowing oneself through shamanic practices, John had the space to express his outstanding commitment as an activist for a better world society based on an economy for life. I served as Expedition Leader in charge of the operation, logistics, itinerary, and PR with the group, harmonizing and sustaining the space so that everyone felt integrated and reinforced. The trip went very well, exceeding the expectations of the passengers and ours.

Since this first trip, I have continued taking groups to Guatemala uninterruptedly every year with John and on my own. Over time, I have gotten to know this beautiful country better and improved our itinerary. I have also developed a close and fraternal relationship with Julio and Tata Domingo. In the second year, Julio asked Tata Domingo to be his mentor, learn the trade of a spiritual leader, or Tata, and acquire strength, knowledge, and practice. After 5 years of intense learning, Julio became Tata and has received the "grace" to continue working with Tata Domingo, his mentor. Having a unique, authentic, legitimate, fantastic work team for Guatemala is a privilege.

The fire ceremonies linked to the 20 Nahuales and the numbers from 1 to 13 combined to form a 260-day calendar called Tzolkin and used for spiritual practices. Therefore, each day of this calendar corresponds to a specific Nahual (energy), which predominates on that day in the real life of the Mayans. Based on this principle, the Nahual present on the day of a person's birth is determined, defining that it is an inherent part of that person's feeling, thinking, and acting; it is almost like a spiritual DNA. From there, a logical-numerical system is developed, by which the nahual present on the day the person was conceived by their parents is also determined; the nahual present in the forging of the person's destiny, and in this way, the person has the opportunity to look at and know themselves. It is an exact, ancestral procedure that is fortunately practiced daily in Guatemala by the Mayan population. In the fire ceremony, a bond is established with the flame. You talk to the fire, speak to it, tell it things about yourself, ask it for answers, and the fire responds in different ways; it shows spirals that form to the right or left. Each direction has a meaning, either through the color of the smoke and in which direction it expands, or through the direction in which the large tobacco located in the center of the altar falls. The responses of fire to the East and North are positive, and to the West and South are negative. The East is linked to the elements of fire, our blood, and our physical appearance. The West, where the sun hides with the element Earth, our rest, death, and dreams. The South with the Water element, with our heart, with what we love, with our feelings. The North, with the element Air, is associated with our thoughts, breathing, and wind.

Note: It has been interesting and significant to see the similarity of meaning in terms of the relationship of the elements with human life between the Mayans and the Jewish tradition. According to the book "The Four Elements of an Empowered Life" by Rav Shlomo Buxbaum:

Earth is the element of the physical body.

Water is the element of emotions and pleasure.

Air is the element of intellect and communication.

Fire is the element of willpower and personal conscience.

The other unique and special space we offer is the nighttime tobacco ceremony in the G complex or Palacio de las Acanaladuras in Tikal, where a giant mask represents the face of a Serpent. Its mouth is formed in a tunnel, with a 1-meter-wide Mayan arch 3 meters high and about 12 meters long. It finally forms a 90-degree angle and continues for an additional 6 meters. Participants enter one by one, with time intervals that allow them to walk in complete darkness inside the tunnel without hearing the footsteps or voices of other people. It is a very intense solo moment. It is so dark that it makes no difference to open or close your eyes, stroll through the tunnel, brush the side walls with your fingers, feel your breathing, and create self-confidence to overcome any feeling of fear and/or apprehension, upon exiting the tunnel you reach a large outdoor rectangle, surrounded by stone structures and giant trees, in silence each person chooses a place to sit or lie down, to see the starry sky and feel the night.

When everyone has entered, they are offered to inhale a bit of Amazonian tobacco water through their nose, which helps them relax, be present, and clear the airways, offering a feeling of lightness and presence. People have their own individual space to be... After a while, Tata Domingo and Tata Julio approach each person with incense, a giant tobacco, and an obsidian or jade knife, and make a cleansing with tobacco smoke, sugar cane alcohol, and the blade (Tijash/cut), which cuts what needs to be eliminated. While the Tatas continue cleaning up, the other people can ask for more tobacco water to inhale. It is a space that intensely contributes to the perception of presence and sacredness, allowing travelers to be intimate with themselves and their search for clarity.

The other unique aspect of Guatemala is exploring the cities abandoned for centuries and invaded by Nature in the Peten jungle. We have accessed unique spaces with nighttime ceremonies of fire and tobacco in Tikal, offerings in Yaxha and Uaxactun, and fire and ritual bathing in Lake Peten Itza, spaces of meditation, clarity, healing, and self-recognition.

Studying the Mayans, it is remarkable that their beginnings were approximately 2000 years BC until the arrival of the Spanish from 1511 to 1697 AD. However, the great collapse occurred when they abandoned large cities and spread across the highlands of Guatemala and the Yucatan Peninsula between 800 and 900 AD. This major collapse was likely due to several factors: a significant drought that caused the loss of political power to the kings and priests, and perhaps health problems due to overpopulation. Today, in Guatemala, there are 22 native languages in the Mayan population, which shows us the great dispersion of the people when they abandoned the big cities.

The analogy with current human civilization is that, despite having developed and mastered the most sophisticated technologies of the time, they overexploited natural resources for the sake of development, just as humans do now, in which, like the Mayans, we have achieved a unique technological development. Still, we have

caused a disproportionate environmental impact, exceeding Nature's self-regenerating ability.

Daniel Koupermann C.

Photos of Guatemala and the Mayan:

1. Tata Domingo

2. Beginning the altar

3. Fire ceremony at Lake Petén Itzá

4. Fire ceremony, Lake Petén Itzá

5. Fire ceremonies at Iximché

6. Beginning the fire ceremony at Iximché

7. Psychonavigation with John Perkins in Tikal

8. Temple of the Jaguar, Tikal

9. Volcán de Agua, Antigua

12. Peru

In 2013, I went to explore Peru to operate a new destination. The topic of the Incas was more familiar to me since it was linked to the historical roots of Ecuador, and I had grown up knowing about them. Likewise, it was closely related to the Andean culture, traditions, and people. I clearly remember my mother taking me to the nine de Octubre market in Cuenca to get cleansed with the women from the medicinal plants section. In the cleansings, you were rubbed with plants and sprayed with puffs of sugar cane alcohol all over the body, especially the head. On my first exploration trip, I "coincidentally" met Jamee in Pisac, a North American colleague who lived in Peru and made holistic trips. We had an excellent connection, so I offered my friends a new destination the following year, choosing the solstice for it. June, which celebrates the Inti Raymi (Festival of the Sun). Jamee helped me with the logistics and guidance; she introduced me to the Pacos, Taitas Queros Sebastián, and Bacilio.

For the second year, I asked Jamee for a high-profile local guide in Andean and Inca culture. That was when I met German Canales, our local guide since then, who also contributed to logistics in the Cusco and Machu Picchu area.

The admirable thing about the Incas is that in just 300 years (1200 AD to 1532 AD, when Atahualpa, the last Inca, was taken prisoner by Francisco Pizarro, the conqueror), they managed to establish an administrative and military domain in a territory of more than 2,000,000 km2. , occupying part of the current republics of Colombia, Ecuador, Peru, Bolivia, Chile, and Argentina. They imposed the Quechua language and political, production, and religious systems.

Even though they were warriors, they paid great attention to learning the technologies and knowledge of the conquered peoples, incorporating them into their system and creating a robust accumulation of knowledge. They built a social fabric between themselves and the incorporated chiefdoms, which allowed them to develop effective political and administrative structures.

Trilogies as a structure of religious principles predominate in the Andean worldview.

The Incas' cosmogonic vision of the world is based on the trilogy of **Hanan Pacha**. In this upper world, the Sun, the moon, the stars, and Viracocha, the creator god, are represented by the Condor. **Kay Pacha** is the world in which we live, with the Apus (Mountains), lakes, rivers, and plant and animal life, and it is represented by the Puma. **The Ukhu Pacha** is the underground world where the ancestors live. It is where knowledge comes from and is represented by the snake.

Another trilogy that expresses fundamental principles of Andean ancestral knowledge is manifested in the Quichua expression **ama killa, ama llula, ama shwa,** "Do not be idle, do not lie, do not steal."

The three laws that govern human life are expressed in another trilogy: **Munay** (Love), **Llankay** (Work), **and Yachay** (Wisdom). These are related to each other. By cultivating Love and Work, we acquire a state of presence and consciousness that gives us Wisdom.

Another of the fundamental principles of the Andean peoples is Reciprocity **(Ayni),** which governs behavior in the relationship between humans at a personal, family, and community level. Give and receive; receiving and giving is the dynamic that allows coexistence in all dimensions. Based on this principle, **Mita** and **Minka** establish a new trilogy. The Mita was the time each citizen worked for the government for a specific time to build roads, palaces, irrigation canals, and general infrastructure works; it was a tribute. The Minka or Minga is the collaboration of the members of a community (collective work), whether for community or family needs.

The Ayni even manifested itself in the conquest of new territories and towns. The Inca first sent emissaries with gifts and offerings to the town chief to be conquered, inviting them to be part of the system. If the proposal was accepted, the conquest and dominion occurred without violence. Otherwise, the invasion would take place militarily, the dominant caste would be annihilated, and the people would be incorporated into the new system to contribute with their skills, knowledge, and tributes. Likewise, the concept of Ayni is used in personal self-evaluation. When doing an act of self-introspection, we analyze how much we have taken from life. (Not how much we have received from life, since it is a passive attitude) versus How much have we given to life? If more has been given than what has been taken, the person achieves the state of Ayni and can access a state of peace and Wisdom. Without Ayni, it is not possible to achieve that state of well-being…

On trips to Peru, we are enveloped in the magic of the incredible and wonderful archeology of the country, which offers ceremonial spaces where we can review the Andean trilogies in our lives and participate in the traditional ceremonies of the Despacho, an offering of gratitude to Pachamama (Mother Earth) for what was received in life that restores Ayni. The Karpay ceremony is an initiation, that is, preparing mentally and emotionally to acquire the ability to feel the presence of the great spirit and receive the "strength" to connect with our spirituality and acquire attributes. It begins with a "cleansing" with stones (huacas) from the Apus (Mountains and Volcanoes), spices, cologne water, tobacco smoke, and other elements.

Tour Machu Picchu, identify its ceremonial context, and discover its monumentality and chosen place, which are closely related to the Incas' spiritual, mystical, and metaphysical connection.

In Peru, we optionally offer ceremonies with Wachuma, the cactus known as San Pedro Trichocereus pachanoi or Echinopsis pachanoi. Which is the power plant of the Andes mountains, identified as a grandfather (masculine energy). It can be ingested day or night and is gentler than Ayahuasca; it does not affect you physically as much, and the way the experience manifests is exceptional. It awakens a detailed and beautiful perception of the natural world if taken during the day. It allows you to focus on self-observation essentials and find answers to self-existential issues.

I last had Wachuma at Shuracpamba in 2018 with Taita Alejo. I was overcome by contemplating Nature at a micro level, observing plants and flowers at a molecular level, until I found a faique tree (acacia macracantha) and placed my right hand on one of its branches to see its lichens. Suddenly, I felt an evident physical sensation in my hand and arm, like a vibration. When I paid attention to the sensation, I realized that the sage from the tree invaded me, like part of my blood. I felt the sage run through my body as if it were my own blood. My relationship with the faique was established at a level of contemplation and total existential integration.

Daniel Koupermann C.

Daniel Koupermann C.

Photos of Peru:

1. Receiving the first sun of the Andean New Year

2. Karpay ceremony

3. Moray

4. Machu Picchu

5. Peruvian Paso horses

6. Sacsayhuamán

7. Walls of Sacsayhuamán

8. Residential sector of Machu Picchu

13. Colombia

In May 2015, I explored Colombia to offer a new destination. The Kogi people in the Sierra Nevada in the Colombian Caribbean attracted me. The Sierra Nevada near Santa Marta is exceptional due to its natural beauty, ancestral peoples, and recent history.

Famous in the 70s for the cultivation of the best marijuana in the world, at that time, the famous *Santa Marta Golden* led to drug trafficking mafias, who violently took over the farms where the Kogi lived. The Kojis were forced to occupy the highest lands away from the plantations. Then, in the '80s and '90s, the farms that grew marijuana changed to the cultivation of coca leaves, which was more profitable but generated the presence of paramilitary groups and FARC guerrillas in the area, who fought each other with blood and violence, which also affected the Kogi, who had to deal with these two groups. They were forced to migrate to even higher lands, where agriculture was not viable. The cold climate makes life much harder.

In 2004, the Colombian Armed Forces began the eradication of all these irregular groups, which lasted until 2012, when the Sierra Nevada area was declared safe and completely free of these illicit activities.

When I went to explore the place to take my groups, I contacted a local guide, Jaruen Rodríguez, who specializes in bird watching, with a lot of experience in the area since he was born in the place and worked as a park ranger in the area of Tayrona National Park, which allowed him to establish contact with some of the Kogi communities in the area. However, when I asked him to help me visit a Kogi community to establish contact and be able to take my travelers, he was reluctant to do so since the indigenous people are very jealous and distrustful of people in general, mainly due to the bad experiences they had during the time of violence and for being very critical of the way non-indigenous Colombians behave by preying on Nature. Jaruen consulted with his Kogi friends about my visit, which was denied. Still, they said that if I was interested in ceremonies with them, they could come down from the mountain to the hotel beach and do the ceremony with my group. Since I had no other option, I accepted that possibility, submitting and following the intuition that told me to take it.

When I finished my exploration, I told John Perkins about my intention to include Colombia in my travels; he was very interested since he had had a coffee farm in the area in the late 70's. The following year, we organized a group trip to Colombia. The itinerary begins in Cartagena, the beauty of its walled city and its fascinating history, for having been the place where, at the time of the conquest, the Spanish sent to Spain all the gold and riches they obtained from Peru, Bolivia, and Ecuador, protecting the city with walls and fortifications, which are the vestiges of the most formidable military architecture on the American continent. Likewise, Cartagena, along with Veracruz in Mexico, were the only African slave markets during that period of history, as well as the headquarters of the fearsome Inquisition, which forced the pagans of the territories under the regime of the Spanish crown to accept the Catholic religion as the only and true one, under penalty of condemnation to torture and death of those who refused to do so. It was also besieged and attacked by pirates and corsairs who sought to obtain the treasures of the conquest. All this, plus the beautiful colonial city, makes a visit to Cartagena a plus on the trip to Colombia.

Then, we continue the trip north along the Caribbean road network, passing through Barranquilla, located on the shores of the Atlantic and at the mouth of the Magdalena River. This vital artery of national commerce is a thriving city famous for its Carnival festivities. I fondly remember it as the place where I lived for two beautiful years of my life, studying there for the last two years of high school.

Then, continuing north towards Santa Marta, you pass through the Ciénega Grande, the largest wetland ecosystem in Colombia, which is nourished by the Atlantic Ocean and the rivers that come down from the Sierra Nevada, especially the branches of the Magdalena River. In this aquatic ecosystem, we visited the community of Nueva Venecia on the west side of the water mirror. Also known as the town of the "water people." Village of stilt houses, where all the houses are literally on the water. People move around in lever canoes or any object that floats; you see children who go to school paddling on a plastic tank cover. There is no sanitary system. The toilets go directly into the lagoon under the houses, where the daily currents linked to the tides recycle and systematically remove all waste from the community every 6 hours.

The only construction on the earth fill is the church and a small part of the school. Next to them, the famous Colombian soccer player Radamel Falcao donated a concrete platform over the lagoon, where a multi-use sports field has been built.

On November 22, 2000, there was a massacre perpetrated by a paramilitary group. They murdered thirty-nine people in Nueva Venecia, many of them in front of the community, and they piled bodies in the small square next to the church. They alleged that there were collaborators from an ELN guerrilla group. Nueva Venecia suffered from the extreme of human violence. The community abandoned the site after the massacre. They returned after two years to restart their lives in their town. A visit to this place shows us the capacity of humans to make a life even in the most challenging conditions. Seeing this on the trip helps us self-evaluate our reality. It contributes to appreciating our own life from an exciting perspective.

We continue north to the area of influence of the Tayrona National Park, where the lush tropical forest combines with the turquoise waters of the Caribbean Sea and the Sierra Nevada de Santa Marta, isolated from the Andes and the highest coastal mountain range, 5,700 m (18,700 ft).) just 42 km (26 mi) from the Caribbean Sea, one of the areas with the highest endemism on the planet. Land of the Kogis, Arhuacos, Kankuamos, and Wiwas, ancestral peoples.

The visit to the Kogis is motivated by their very particular vision of the world and how they relate to life. They communicate with Nature, and their wise men promote the planet's healing through their understanding and knowledge. Additionally, due to their history of having lived through years of violence and the interference of dark forces in their territory, and of having experienced the consequences of "human wretchedness." They consider themselves the elder brothers, and we, the inhabitants of the modern world, the younger brothers, for whom they have a message to communicate. The younger brothers (us) eat, drink water, breathe air, see beauty, live, and give no thanks. We extract coal, gold, and minerals, cultivate and harvest the land, fish, work, and... give no thanks. The younger brothers are as if asleep, dominated, and entertained by matters unrelated to taking care of Nature, taking care of Creation, which are what humans were created or materialized for.

The Kogis' political organization is based on traditional laws. They are governed by their wise men (Mamos), most of whom live in the high parts of the Sierra.

On the first trip, we did as they had said; we stayed at Ecohabs, a hotel inside Tayrona Park. Near the hotel beach is the mouth of an estuary, where one of the altars is on the black line. This imaginary line surrounds the Kogi territory. The altar is called "the nine stones". A group of 8 Kogis arrived at the hotel with two Mamos, a boy of about 6 years old, and a friend of Jaruen who was a community leader.

We walked along the beach to the altar and did a ceremony or ¨pagamento¨ payment.

The Mamo gives the child some cotton balls so that he can give two to each participant. The idea is to hold each cotton ball in your hands between the index finger and thumb and move the cotton balls circularly while bringing to mind the thoughts and emotions related to the reason for the ceremony and/or the attribute of the altar where the ceremony is done. Negative, painful, uncomfortable, and distressing thoughts and emotions are brought up if the ceremony is to cleanse oneself to lighten those negative burdens. Or if the ceremony's purpose is to express gratitude for a favor received, in short…purposes and purposes. The meaning of these ceremonies is so powerful that we can offer our suffering as a payment (offering) to Mother Nature. Then, the child collects the cotton balls from each participant and gives them to the Mamo, who places them as an offering on the altar or hides them in a crevice on the rocks.

Several altars along this black line run through the territory, from the high peaks of the Sierra Nevada to the beaches and reefs, forming a perimeter that covers part of the departments of Magdalena, Guajira, and Cesar.

At the end of the ceremony, I asked the Mamo for permission to make an offering at the altar of the nine stones with chopped Amazonian tobacco leaves I had brought from Ecuador. The Mamo authorized me, so I opened the bag of tobacco and invited the group members to take some and make offerings on the altar one by one, taking the necessary time to do so. While I offered the tobacco, I began to sing my Icarus. The offering took its time due to the size of the group. When everyone finished, I offered the Mamo my tobacco so he could make the offering like everyone else; the Mamo and the other Kogi did, and we closed the space spontaneously and shared. As we said goodbye, the Mamo told me: If you return next year with your friends, you will be welcome to visit us in our community. Grandfather Tobacco allowed me to offer enough confidence to be accepted and welcomed.

Since then, we have visited Kogi communities for several years, strengthening our relationship. When we see the Kogis and learn about their worldview, that profoundly impacts us; since the priority in their lives is simply to conserve and preserve Nature, they are happy with simple community life. They have no desire to accumulate wealth. They live to read and listen to Mother Nature through her language in rain, winds, lightning, and thunder; they suffer deeply from the destruction of habitats and from humanity's greed to permanently exploit the Earth's resources.

In their mythology, everything existed spiritually at the beginning of time, when the Mothers and Fathers decided to materialize it. They materialized the Earth, its mountains and valleys; they materialized the waters in all their forms, the sun, the moon, the stars, the air, the animals, and they admired the beauty and perfection of what was created; then, they decided to materialize humans, with the sole purpose of taking care of what is materialized, being custodians of creation, was the only mission of humans. And so it was, until one day, a group of humans began to get distracted from their mission, making tools. The Fathers and Mothers were amazed to see how happy these humans felt making objects and tools, so they took them away from the Kogis and the Sierra Nevada and took them to the other side of the ocean, where they stayed and continued doing things. These are the so-called younger brothers; the Kogis, who stayed behind to fulfill the mission entrusted to them, are the older brothers.

The Sierra Nevada de Santa Marta, their land, is the center and origin of this materialization. Its peaks are connected by invisible threads with all the mountains, lakes, rivers, oceans, and energy vortexes on the planet, the solar system, and the universe. The Sierra Nevada is surrounded by the imaginary black line, which peripherally defines a territory that goes from the snowy peaks and foothills to the beach line and reefs in the Caribbean Sea.

The Kogi maintain that the actions and interactions of all organic and inorganic beings and the thoughts of humans feed Mother Earth, so the quality of thoughts is directly related to the quality of food that Nature receives.

The most used practice to generate good and positive thoughts is through Payments, that is, offerings to pay back to life for what has been received: health, food, well-being, family, beauty, joys, and sufferings. The offerings are made mainly with cotton balls, made only by children between 5 and 7 years of age. These are delivered to the offerers, who place the cotton balls between the fingers of the hand.

While they move the little specks between their fingers, they bring the thoughts one offers to the moment, always profoundly grateful for what they have received.

These offerings are made in particular sites located on the black line or the internal lines (meridians that descend from the peaks to the beach), where these sites are like altars, which are natural formations in the territory. The mouths of the rivers in the Caribbean, the lagoons of the Sierra, natural formations on the coast, giant stones with petroglyphs, and hot springs are the altars where the Pagamentos or payments are made. Each of these altars has a particular attribute with which the offering is linked.

If you want to see, feel, and know your spirit, observe your thoughts; there, the spirit manifests. Kogi statement.

It has moved me to meet them and learn from them. The same happens with the travelers I take to their territory; it sensitizes them to their vision of themselves and awakens deep admiration and solidarity.

Something extraordinary has been happening with the groups that we take to Colombia. By knowing and listening to how the Kogis were forced to abandon their ancestral lands, they become aware and show solidarity. When they return to their country, they organize to raise funds with different activities and initiatives in such a way that the following year, when a new group ends, representatives of the previous year's group arrive with the money collected, with which they buy farms from settlers in Kogi territory, many of them with sacred sites inside.

After the purchase of the land or the community works in which the donation money is invested, we make a pilgrimage of gratitude with the Kogis, for whom it is an obligation at least once in their life to visit the sites. Sacred sites in the territory within the "black line" and make payments in said sites. In these pilgrimages that we have made every time we receive a donation, we invite at least 10 to 12 Kogis to realize that dream, since, in modern times, it is difficult and expensive to get around and visit the scattered sites in the territory.

The land will be used according to the agreement with the Colombian government, which states that 30% will be used for agricultural crops and 70% for conservation. The Kogi have once again become guardians of their ancestral lands.

Pilgrimage 2017 $ 9,515 US Farrah Garan

Two plots of land were purchased using the money raised by the 2016 group. One plot will be used primarily for agriculture. The second plot of land sits at the base of a hill sacred to the Kogi community. The Kogis will use this land to gather materials to build a ceremonial structure on the hill and as a buffer so that no other construction can compromise this sacred area. Our funds enabled the Kogi to acquire 19.77 acres of land in total (8 hectares)

Pilgrimage 2018 $6,800 US Jaime Schmitz

Rebuilt the communal house for men and the communal house for the women with solar panels and a battery bank to allow the ladies to weave "Shigras", as a primary source of economic income for the families.

Pilgrimage 2019 $14,000 US Tom MacGibbon

We can all learn from the Kogi what it is to be true earth keepers, stewards of the land, deeply connected to all beings and all life.

We were able to acquire two farms totaling 53 hectares (130 acres) of land, which the Kogi had dreamed of purchasing, yet had to learn how it would happen. The land we bought is next to a small community where the only space available is for the 30 huts and one small school.

The land will benefit 25 families, approximately 125 Kogi in total.

Daniel Koupermann C.

Photos of Colombia:

1. Kogi celebration

2. The Cherwa community receiving a 40-hectare property

3. Mamo Alejandro and Daniel at a Tairona ceremonial site

4. Mamo Lorenzo

5. The Kogi community of Duanamake

6. Contemplation during an offering at Cerro Kennedy

7. Mamo Marco

8. Mamo Juan and a group of Kogis on pilgrimage

9. Kogi women during our pilgrimage

10. Offering during the pilgrimage at an altar on the Black Line

11. Offering with Mamo Lorenzo

12. Pagamento at the upper slopes of Cerro Kennedy, Sierra Nevada

13. Offering at an altar on the Black Line

14. Kogi pilgrimage

15. Offering site at the stones of Duaname

16. Tom MacGibbon and Daniel with a leader and mamo in the Cherwa community

14. Patagonia

The next destination I opened for my travels was Patagonia. This land always caught my attention. In 2017, I explored with my wife, Linda, and friends. I had been to Buenos Aires on two previous occasions for work when I was in CANODROS, without the time to get to know this beautiful and great city. Its European architecture and the idiosyncrasies of its people make it unique and reflect the migration of Italians, Spaniards, Croatians, and Czechoslovakians at a time when Europe suffered from wars and famines. It is a fascinating city that invites you to discover its charms.

One of the most outstanding characteristics is the Milongas, where tango is cultivated uninterruptedly. I was very attracted to tango; I always remember my parents, who danced with great skill in my childhood memories. I remember one occasion in a Cuban restaurant in Miami called Los Violines, where my parents went out to dance the tango with so much passion and dedication that, at one point, the other people dancing there made a ring around them, and the room was filled with applause. It was the only time I remember my mother blushing.

Milongas are the temples of tango, where ordinary people go to dance and where traditions and rituals persist almost untouched to this day.

Married and engaged couples go, but also many single men and women who don't know each other, with the sole purpose of finding someone to dance with. Couples are placed on one side of the dance floor, single women on the other, and single men in front. They observe each other carefully, trying to choose who to dance with. Single men, with great prudence and discretion, try to make eye contact with the woman they would like to dance with. Still, for fear of being publicly rejected and embarrassed, they do not dare to stand up and extend their hand, inviting the women, so once eye contact has been established, with great discretion, the man points with his eyes to the dance floor. If the woman smiles and nods, it is a sign that the invitation has been accepted. Still, suppose the woman does not smile and looks away. In that case, the gentleman knows immediately that he must look for another partner. When I take clients to the Milongas, the observation of this ritual is fascinating and evident.

What catches our attention the most is that once they go out dancing, without having met before, their dance skills are impressive, giving the impression that they have been dancing together for years. Truly fascinating. We receive tango classes before going to the Milonga, so that if someone feels motivated to dance, they have a basic idea of how to do it. Understand that tango has 4 and 8 beats in its rhythm, that the dancers must hold their chests together, that it is the man who directs and proposes the movements, and that the woman must let herself go, and that there is a base of obligatory movements that each couple executes in their own way. These are sufficient basic principles to try to dance tango.

From Buenos Aires to Calafate, a city located in the South of

Argentina, a place of unique and particular beauty, and our first encounter with Patagonia, the land where the Southern Patagonian Ice Field is also known as Patagonian Continental Ice, which is the third largest area of continental ice in the world, behind Antarctica and Greenland. It is one of the largest reserves of fresh water on Earth. It plays a vital role in regulating and cooling the planet's atmospheric temperature.

Likewise, the region on the Globe is located between 40 and 60 degrees south latitude. The intense and powerful winds known to marine navigators as the mighty 40s predominate all year round. These winds circle the planet at that latitude all year round. The only obstacles they encounter along their path are some not-very-high mountains in New Zealand and the Patagonian Andes, where they condense, producing snowfall in the high parts. After 15 years, the snowfall becomes ice, which gives rise to glaciers.

Arriving at Calafate from the airport, we depart directly for 3 hours north to Chaltèn, a small city within the Los Glaciares National Park, with a protected natural area, considered a mecca for fans of hiking and mountaineering. Fitz Roy (3,405 meters/11,171 feet) is the most representative mountain due to its beauty and the places that surround it. We stayed two nights in the area doing walks and horseback riding, which put us in contact with this privileged place's natural beauty and energy. The town is extraordinary because of the many visitors who come year-round. It has a relaxed atmosphere with cafes, restaurants, bars, and accommodations for all tastes and budgets.

We return to Calafate, where we also stay for two nights. We sail on the Argentine lake with its hanging glaciers, the most iconic of which is the Perito Moreno glacier, where we disembark, and which arouses admiration for its dimensions and natural beauty. It is impressive to see this river of ice from the shore that descends and breaks in the lake's water, causing impressive noises. The place's natural beauty is overwhelming; it makes us feel small and part of something bigger.

We continue by land towards the South, entering the Patagonian steppe with its particular ecosystems, where we see large herds of guanacos (*Lama guanicoe*) and where you can see the magnificent Andean Condor (*Vultur gryphus*), the largest flying bird in the world. We crossed the border to Chile, and little by little, we felt the transition from dry Argentine Patagonia to the Chilean Patagonia that is wetter, greener, and closer to the Andes mountain range and the Pacific Ocean, to reach the Torres del Paine National Park, another place iconic in Patagonia, equally famous for its natural beauty and its mountain system, where fog, rain, and sun magically combine to once again marvel us. We take short walks and van tours along its trails and valleys; with some luck, we can observe the Puma (*Puma concolor*) in the wild, making this place its natural habitat with important populations of large cats.

We leave Patagonia, flying from Puerto Natales to Santiago, the capital of Chile, to learn about its history and monumentality. Visiting the central market and tasting Chilean seafood is vital to this exciting city's identity.

We also delve into the country's winemaking tradition for a day.

We visit the Casablanca valley and its vineyards, where expert oenologists introduce us to winemaking and taste delicious wines.

Personal search and healing occur through contemplation and contact with Nature, its power, and beauty on this journey.

The trips I have shared have been my job and an essential part of my way of life. They have also been a source of permanent learning due to the diversity of people who have participated, the knowledge and practices of the indigenous cultures of the countries visited, and the ceremonial spaces involved in each of them. The benefit level for travelers depends solely on each participant's dedication, presence, and intention. However, I humbly recognize that I have witnessed significant personal transformations in my clients through travel and contact with indigenous cultures. That is why, for me, the work done became, in the last 20-25 years, not only a way of subsistence but also my mission in life, contributing to others and my personal growth.

Daniel Koupermann C.

Daniel Koupermann C.

The Invisible Journey

Daniel Koupermann C.

Photos of Patagonia:

1. Sunrise at Torres del Paine

2. Hike to Fitz Roy

3. Fitz Roy

4. Horseback riding at Nibepo Aike

5. Southern hike at Perito Moreno

6. Condor at Perito Moreno

7. Andes range and Lake Argentino from Puente del Yate

8. Iceberg on Lake Argentino

9. 4x4 excursion in El Calafate

10. Fitz Roy, El Chaltén

11. Perito Moreno Glacier viewpoint

12. Hanging glacier, Lake Argentino

13. Perito Moreno Glacier walkways

14. Iceberg on Lake Argentino

15. Puerto Vacas

16. Laguna Capri, El Chaltén

17. Penguin colony, Ushuaia

18. Ushuaia

19. Milonga in Buenos Aires

20. Kayaking in Bariloche

15. Women

What we learn comes from many sources; important learnings come from our relationships with the women in our lives and with our friends; that is why I share these memories.

When I think about women in my life, the first image that comes to me is that of my beloved Mother, Doña Yoli, from whom I have received an essential part of my formation as a person and a man. A woman of strong character who always supported us in our home and supported our father in his vicissitudes. She gave me the guidelines to understand life in its proper perspective. Loving, but equally solid and strict when I misbehaved. She was by my side, consoling or congratulating me at every stage of my life. She taught me to see the positive and negative sides of human relationships. I am so grateful to have had a mother and teacher like Doña Yoli.

My sisters, Giselle and Paulette, developed in me filial love and the sense of feeling somehow responsible for their well-being. Giselle is so sensitive and fragile, but simultaneously full of love and greatness as a mother and a great worker. Just like Doña Yoli, she is the one who maintains the space of her home. Paulette, on the other hand, is a child of the war who suffered so much, not only due to the violence of the conflict in World War II, but also as a victim of the

Nazis' irrational hatred for the Jews. Her traumas marked her for her entire life. However, she taught us a lesson about survival.

My childhood and teenage loves contributed something beautiful and unique that made me a romantic lover. They are always remembered with special care and affection.

Sarita, my first wife and the mother of my three children, took me to the extremes of love, total happiness, and the deepest pain. Twenty-five years of living together, experiencing everything involved in marriage. We continue together in life as parents and as friends. I thank her infinitely for giving me my children, the greatest blessing received in life, a source of permanent inspiration, and Najes (a word in Yiddish that does not exist in any other language and that means the sum of feelings that only children and grandchildren give us). In other languages, generic words such as unconditional love, pride, tenderness, and inspiration are used. Still, there is no specific word that means and reflects that reality. Since I became a father, I have had the grace to always be full of Najes. Thank you, beloved children!

María Dolores, whom I met by chance after 32 years of being in love as a teenager. She was the one who healed the pain of my divorce and made me excited again about love. Unfortunately, after 2 ½ years of a relationship, she suffered a terrible stroke, which caused severe, irreversible injuries. We have remained linked and communicated. I visit her occasionally. A beautiful and unforgettable love.

When this tragedy happened, I understood that my destiny was not to be accompanied by any woman in my life. After the divorce and stroke, it became clear to me that I needed to be alone. I lived in Puyo working for the Achuar Air Service, resigned to being alone without a partner, without a cohabitant, and I connected with that scenario, resigned, convinced.

Suddenly, without thinking about it, asking for it, or wishing for it, Linda, my current wife, appeared. A former passenger on a trip to the jungle who came to Ecuador to learn Spanish during her sabbatical year. She is ten years older than me and from a different culture. Little by little, she filled the void that I had emotionally. A mature woman with a lot of world, who was also looking for something and/or someone to break the loneliness of many years, to change paradigms of a life dedicated mainly to work, to find someone to accompany and sustain her soul, that is, with the same existential need that I was experiencing at that moment.

She won my heart and that of my children; her authentic and unconditional generosity and contribution to our well-being made her part of us. We have lived together for 20 years, of which 18 have been married. She is a good friend of Sarita, the mother of my children. She has created and sustained a space where we can all be together and celebrate the feeling of family to the fullest. It is great love, an adult, free love, where you live what is essential, what is important, without allowing the mundane things of life to interfere with the art of loving. Thanks, Linda!

16. Friends

What would life be like without friends, so much time, and so much life we spend with them? So many experiences and life lessons were received from friends without having that intention, just sharing life with them and, over time, understanding so many things about our humanity and what people are like. From friends, we learn and experience loyalty, envy, solidarity, betrayal, deception, affection, the superfluous, the profound, hypocrisy, etc. Friends are a powerful source of knowledge in our lives.

There are friends from school with whom contact was lost after so many years. One of them who was always close is Pancho (el negro) Serrano, with whom, until his death, we maintained a close relationship. From adolescence, Pablito Abad, a gentleman friend, excellent musician, and singer, symbolizes unconditional loyalty. Juan Cobos, the rebel and critic of life. Diego (Chino) Alarcón, the experienced one, is always taking risks. All of them are deceased and missed. The dear friends of the "Bomba" group, with whom we met every night on a neighborhood corner, talk about motorcycles, cars, soccer, girls, and gossip in general. Pablo (el negro) Martínez, the persistent one with iron will and determination, is a consummate poet. Esteban and Silvia, Ernesto and María Inés, close friends, couples always and forever, with whom we enjoy friendship in our older years, adorned with the company of Ernesto (Cuchucho) Aguilar, who evolved from an icon of good humor to a profound philosopher and photographer.

My dear friends from the Hebrew Unión school in Barranquilla, with whom, in just 2 years, sharing the classroom, a friendship was founded that has lasted from then until now, through distance, always present on birthdays, in religious celebrations, constantly reviving memories and feelings of friendship.

Through my work on travel, I have also gained great and dear friends. Julio and Tata Domingo in Guatemala, Jaruen and Lucy in Colombia, Germán in Peru, Sumpa, Taish, Celestino, Simón, Chikuish, and Manari in the Amazon, are co-workers and an essential part of life.

María Belén Páez is a dear and endearing friend whom I met as a candidate for naturalist guide in Kapawi, who, over time, has become a leader and activist in the defense of the Amazon and indigenous peoples, recognized worldwide. Her charisma, knowledge, and deep commitment to the causes she fights for inspire me.

I also have Bill and Lynne Twist and John Perkins, special friends with whom we have developed our friendship linked to our commitment to protecting the Amazon and contributing to the self-determination of Indigenous peoples in general and the Amazon in particular. The Twists, together with María Belén, have been the catalysts for the work of The Pachamama Alliance and the Pachamama Foundation, the consequences of which have allowed the achievement of magnificent results in the search for a better world.

Since I was 50 years old when I married Linda, life has given me dear friends, Joel and Judy, Víctor and Lindy, Saúl and Dianne, and Gary, with whom we share life in our older years, where only what is essential is lived, where you only give, where nothing is expected in return.

Fortunately, I have many other friends who brighten my life. They have not been mentioned, are not intimate, and appear occasionally. Still, they have significant meaning and nourish and brighten my life.

Daniel Koupermann C.

Photos of Friends:

1. Manari, Daniel, and Rodrigo in Sapara territory

2. JP and DK, January 2024

3. Pablito Abad, the musician

4. Pancho Serrano and Daniel in Olón

5. Pablito Abad – Sentimiento

6. Classmates from Colegio Hebreo Unión, Barranquilla, Colombia

7. Daniel, Belén, Sara, John, Bill, and Lynne (The Pachamama Alliance)

8. Daniel with Shaman Taish Wayusentsa

9. The Four Musketeers: Esteban, Ernesto, Cuchucho, and Daniel

10. Etsa, Daniel, and Yaur in Kuzutkau

11. Jaruen and Lucy, my beloved guides and friends in Colombia

12. Lindy, Linda, Victor, Judy, Joel, and Daniel in the Redwoods

17. The Teachings

Here, I share some of the teachings I have received, which I have shared with my children because I consider them essential for understanding vital situations in our lives.

Readers may not accept some of them as valid. They may even cause rejection and annoyance because they conflict with beliefs or life experiences. However, they have been valid for me since I have had the opportunity to verify them in my own life.

Our mind and intelligence are the most precious gifts that Nature has given us as a species. Yet, they are also the biggest obstacles to our spiritual growth and development.

It permanently produces ideas, many of them based on or stimulated by premises and assumptions. These ideas are a product of wrong information, ignorance, beliefs, and unrealized hidden desires. They affect our state of mind and can make us erroneously perceive reality and make inappropriate decisions. I call this whirlwind of ideas and thoughts noise.

That is why we have heard that we must calm our minds and listen to our hearts to make crucial decisions. The heart is literally a muscle, so to understand the true meaning of our "heart," there is a teaching that shows this relationship simply.

To continue, it is essential to mention what Dr. Albert Einstein explained when discussing what he calls "the fields." One of the best-known examples is that of the electromagnetic field, from which we understand that the moment there is electricity, there is naturally magnetism and vice versa; that is, they exist together, and simultaneously, their Nature is shared. In the same way, we must understand the relationship between mind and heart; they form a single field, and they equally owe each other being co-natural; they cannot be separated.

Our mind: the teaching says that our mind is like a circle, filled with dense and thick gray matter, with a tiny red dot in its center, our heart. As children, we go through life with our minds, receiving experiences, family, school, friends, career, and life; most experiences enter our mind and get trapped somewhere in the thick gray matter, some closer to the outside, others a little deeper, some inclined to one side or the other, others straight. But none penetrate far enough to the center to touch the red dot (our heart). When this happens (touch the red dot), the experience bounces back inside the gray circle, marking a pink line. The more experiences we allow to touch the red dot, the more pink lines we mark, and the more pink lines we make, the less thick the gray matter becomes. It becomes a better conductor, allowing more and more experiences to touch the red dot. Eventually, there will be less gray and more pink in our minds, and we will live more with our hearts. When I received this teaching, I was 50 years old; I seriously and in detail analyzed my own life to understand how many experiences had touched my red point, having had such an intense life with such varied moments and emotions. I was amazed to discover that in 50 years of life, only five experiences had touched my heart: the birth of each of my children, the death of my father, and the divorce of the mother of my children… What a surprise, what a discovery. Then, I became aware that our mind does not allow this necessary and convenient thing to happen to us. He taught me to educate my mind, to calm the noise it produces, and not allow any idea or thought to disturb my peace of mind. Little by little, in years of work, I have kept this teaching present and will continue to do so until the end of my life. My mind accompanies me better, contributes to my well-being, and allows me to approach my spirituality without noise and distractions.

This teaching is reaffirmed by what was learned from the Kogis in the Sierra Nevada de Santa Marta in Colombia, who say: *If you want to see and know your spirit, observe your thoughts.*

My different selves: This teaching is based on observation, the only way to identify my other selves. In the academy, they are called ego, personality, and superego; in the teaching received, they are called entities.

These entities develop in us as we go through our lives. They are various and mighty since we feel and respond to life circumstances through them. They know us like no one else; they know everything about us and our lives, and that is why they have the power to manipulate us and subdue our authentic and unique selves.

Daniel Koupermann C.

In my personal case, there is a Daniel who was addicted to work, and when he was working, he forgot everything. This one dominated my life in those moments since he was only interested in satisfying his interest. There was another Daniel who liked sex too much. In those moments, he dominated, making me lose all perspective and immersing me in an animalistic way in the world of pleasure and sexual fantasies. He was only interested in doing his thing. Another Daniel was a friend, a drinker, a smoker, a loudmouth, and when he was with friends, he dominated and satisfied their interests. Another Daniel liked being a father, hugging his children, and feeling tenderness. He dominated my moment when I was with my children. Another Daniel victimized himself, and another overvalued himself and was totally egocentric. These Daniels were so different from each other, with such dissimilar interests and behaviors, thoughts and desires... my different selves, which made me live dispersed and in permanent conflict with myself. Those mentioned are only a few of all the Daniels that lived in me. So they taught me to observe myself carefully, which of those Daniels spoke, thought, and acted at this or that moment and circumstance. By carefully observing myself, I could catch them red-handed again and again until I had fully identified each of them. Once this is achieved, you can stop feeding them, and they disappear due to starvation. The final objective is to allow one to unify and be the authentic Daniel, the only Daniel, the owner of the house, the one who works, enjoys sex, friends, and fatherhood, sees himself with all the limitations we have, and discovers and lives humbly, without pretensions, authentically and detached from the story we have invented about ourselves.

• **Building the soul:** I felt terrible resistance when I received this. It was almost like listening to a heresy since it went against all the education I had received on the matter and my beliefs about the human soul. I am sure that many readers may have a similar reaction.

However, I processed it and contrasted it with my observations of examples in history and life until I accepted it in my heart as a truth.

The teaching says that when born healthy and complete, we come into the world with all the necessary equipment and tools (divine breath) to build our souls. Therefore, believing that all humans are born with a soul is inaccurate. For example, characters in history like Hitler, Stalin, Duvalier, and others who caused millions of people so much pain and misery did not manage to build their souls. Did they have souls?

The teaching tells us that in the field where we live, there are thousands of variables and only two constants: the beauty of Nature and human Misery. The beauty of Nature will always be present. At the same time, the variables will change, rotate, and appear recurrently or for the first time, but there will be many.

In that field where we make our lives, with those two constants and thousands of variables, we have to build our soul, which is the only thing we have to transcend...?

• **The invented story:** Since we are aware of and memorize the experiences of our lives, we invent a story about ourselves based on actual events but conceived through our own interpretation of the facts. That my father was like that, that my mother taught me this or that thing, that I suffered when I was at school for this or that, that I chose this career for this or that reason, that I suffered when such a lover abandoned me, that I was thrilled when I had this experience, etc., etc. The story we invent about ourselves makes us act, feel, perceive, and make decisions with specific parameters that are a consequence of that story.

That is why we are the way we are and why, most of the time, we obtain more or less the same results at different times in our lives.

So, suppose we want to obtain different results at some point in life. In that case, we must put aside that invented story about ourselves.

For this, the teaching tells us that from our skin inside, it is inside, and from our skin outside, it is outside. And it says that the world is empty and meaningless; out there, things simply are. They are neither pretty nor ugly, green or red, small or big; they simply are what they are. We give them meaning, definition, and concept, but they simply are.

So, to create a new possibility for us that is not linked to our history, we have to go out there, where the world is empty and meaningless, and from there, create a new possibility for us that will be different and not related to the linked parameters to the invented story about ourselves, which throughout our lives has made us obtain more or less the same results. Only in this way will we get different results…

The appropriate position: To pray, meditate, and make important decisions, it is necessary to assume the proper position in which we place our intellectual, rational center at the same level as our emotional center in such a way that neither of the two predominates. To achieve this, we must consciously and voluntarily concentrate on this idea and balance these two centers at that moment. Only then will we be in the ideal position to pray, meditate, and make crucial decisions.

According to Jewish tradition, this is the intention of tying the leather ribbons on our left arm and around our heads when we put on the Tefilim (phylacteries) to pray and fulfill a vital mitzvah (precept).

Ayni means reciprocity in Quichua and is a fundamental principle in Andean culture.

The teaching says: In life, we must periodically evaluate our personal Ayni, comparing when we have taken (not received) from life and how much we have given to life. When we take more than we give, there is no Ayni. When we take the same as we give, there is no Ayni. When we give more than we take, there is Ayni. Only when there is Ayni can we access happiness and wisdom.

The relationship between take and give is not one-to-one. If I earn $1,000 in a business, it does not mean I should provide that same value in exchange. But I must "give" with the right attitude; taking care of my plants and animals, doing charity as much as possible, making offerings of gratitude, helping others, contributing to community work, or any type of work that contributes to generating well-being around me.

We use the verb to take and not to receive because receiving puts us in a passive attitude and position, while taking or holding places us in an active position and responsibility for our actions.

In the Andean culture, this principle is manifested, for example, in Minka or Minga, which is voluntary collective work within a community or a region. When everyone helps build a house for a newly married couple, or to build an irrigation system, a road, or to clear a community boundary.

Also, based on this principle, in the time of the Incas, when the king wanted to conquer a territory, he first sent his emissaries with meaningful gifts and offerings to the lord of the territory to be conquered to peacefully request that he join the Inca government and system. If the gifts were accepted, the incorporation into the Inca Empire took place peacefully. In the case of rejecting the offerings, military force was used, killing the lord of the conquered lands while respecting the rest of the population.

Likewise, in the Inca, all infrastructure works, such as roads, temples, administrative collections, and storage centers, were built with the collaboration of the population, who gave a third of their time annually for this objective as reciprocity to the system of life that welcomed them and provided everything necessary. It was voluntary work; in the Inca times, there was no slavery.

Maintain your center: Do not argue with fools and ignorant people, lest you also become like them.

The halftones: One law regulating everything is the so-called "Law of Interruption," which maintains that everything is interrupted. A growing plant is in itself an interruption. This law is reaffirmed in the musical staff, since between the notes Mi and Fa and between Fi and Do, there is an interruption, which is musically overcome with the so-called halftones, which allow the musical harmony to continue flowing.

So in our lives, interruptions are permanent and of all kinds, from when a tire goes down on the car, or when the vehicle doesn't start, or when we miss an appointment, or when a plate breaks, A friend or family member dies, or there are so many possibilities of finding interruptions in our lives, therefore, as in music, we must learn to produce halftones in our lives. There are also thousands of options for producing halftones, depending on the interruption and the circumstances. For example, if we disagree with our partner, it could be a smile, a flower, a hug, or an apology. If our boss behaves unfairly or rudely, understand that it is his problem and do not allow it to affect and hurt us; remain silent and be resilient, etc. Depending on each case, we can always generate the halftone necessary to overcome the interruption.

Meditation Exercise: Look at the Nature around you. Start stripping it of its dimension of time and space. Do this by sending the object of your observation to your youth, childhood, birth, and conception. In the case of a plant, bring it to its seed stage. In the case of a building, return it to the original drawing board. And go further. Allow yourself to reduce the plant to its potential state within the parent tree and the architectural drawing to the concept state. Understand that this process is valid for everything. Through this approach, you can live daily in wonder and deep appreciation due to your conscious awareness and respect for the Nature of Creation.

By Rabbi Laibl Wolf, renowned mystic, author, and speaker on Kabbalah topics. He currently resides in Melbourne, Australia.

My Invocation

I invite the reader to look at their life as a whole, to be overwhelmed by everything they have experienced, to give enough value to what they have received, and with that, perhaps consider starting their invisible journey, their return journey, to offer their ego to life now that we are whole with all our abilities now! Do not wait until we are old and incapable of caring for ourselves, when we may have to sacrifice our ego.

I share this work, representing my visible journey, outward journey, and my life until now. I cannot guarantee that my invisible journey will begin, the return journey, because if I believe it, it means I have not started it. I only know that I live daily with that teaching, trying to be present, feeling complete, and happy. I don't need anything; everything I have is perfect and enough.

I don't need to learn anything else of my will; I keep learning because life continues teaching, and I am awake, attentive, happy, and complete.

THANK YOU!

Daniel Koupermann C.